ETHNIC CHRONOLOGY SERIES
NUMBER 18

The Hungarians in America
1583-1974
A Chronology & Fact Book

Compiled and edited by

Joseph Széplaki

1975
OCEANA PUBLICATIONS, INC.
DOBBS FERRY, NEW YORK

Library of Congress Cataloging in Publication Data

Széplaki, Joseph
    The Hungarians in America, 1583-1974

    (Ethnic chronology series ; no. 18)
    Bibliography: p.
    Includes index.
    1. Hungarian Americans. I. Title. II. Series.
E184.H95S86   973'.04'94511   75-11505
ISBN 0-379-00514-X

Manufactured in the United States of America

TO MY CHILDREN

VICTOR AND ANIKÓ

TABLE OF CONTENTS

"Never consider an immigrant to become a
loyal American citizen, unless he retains
his love for his motherland."
Abraham Lincoln

EDITOR'S FOREWORD

Every immigrant lives in a divided world partly by choice and largely
of necessity. He divides his attention between the social, political, and
cultural phenomena of two countries. He is ineluctably bound to his native
land even as he tries to prove loyal, receptive, and responsive to his adopted country. Thus he is very sensitive to the customs, institutions, and
events in both countries. This duality is reflected and attested by this
short study.

There are comparatively few Hungarians living at home and abroad.
According to the latest statistical figures, the total population of present-
day Hungary is nearly ten million, and there are nearly five million scattered throughout the world. Of the expatriates less than one million live
in North America. Yet Hungarians have exerted influence on American
society out of proportion to their numbers. The Hungarian War of Independence of 1848-49, Louis Kossuth's American journey, and the Hungarian
Revolution of 1956 have left their mark on America and Americans. The
individual achievements of Hungarians living in America are also noteworthy. Professor Albert Szent-Györgyi, the Hungarian scientist and winner
of the Nobel prize in medicine and physiology, notes in the introduction to
the 1966 edition of <u>Hungarians</u> <u>in</u> <u>America</u>: <u>A</u> <u>Biographical</u> <u>Directory</u> <u>of</u>
<u>Professionals</u> <u>of</u> <u>Hungarian</u> <u>Origin</u> <u>in</u> <u>the</u> <u>Americas</u>:

> The number and quality of these people surprised
> the world. Many of America's leading musicians
> are Hungarians, and so are many of its scientists,
> architects, etc. The development of the atomic
> bomb, which opened a new chapter in human history,
> and was meant to defend liberty, is linked to a great
> extent, to the names of four Hungarians.

A Hungarian, by his nature, is of an intellectual, individualistic, and
critical frame of mind. Hungarians in America have threfore banded together in many hundreds of autonomous and independent associations instead
of one or several huge organizations. This is why it is impossibe to give
in this thin volume a complete picture of the life of Hungarian Americans.
My primary objective as an editor is to provide a selected but balanced list
of Hungarian Americans and their contributions to American society in important fields of endeavor. The demarcation of the fields, the choice of per-

sons and their achievements, and the mode of presentation may seem arbitrary but are really inevitable. Other editors of similar orientation may come up with slightly different selections as well as a different arrangement of the data.

This book consists, aside from this introduction, of five parts named Chronology, Documents, Appendices, Bibliographical Aid, and Name Index. The Chronology presents - year by year, in concise and largely self-contained entries - persons, groups, institutions, publications, as well as historical, social, and economic events pertaining to the history of Hungarian Americans or to the historical-cultrual relations between the United States and Hungary. The subheadings in the Table of Contents (see p.   ) reveal the classification I have attempted to employ within the chronological mode of presentation, but I must warn the user that the classification is far from watertight precisely because of the many-sidedness of the chronologically presented historical data. Many, if not all, of the entries could be presented under practically any other existing subheading; in fact, all of the entries could be presented under altogether different subheadings. In other words, the subheadings in the Table of Contents merely reflect my interpretation of major trends suggested by the data and are not intended to obscure concurrent minor trends equally suggested by them.

The documents, appendices, bibliographical aid, and name index are intended to serve partly as documentation and partly as reference material for beginning, intermediate, and advanced students. I sincerely hope that some of them will correct, amplify, and extend the work I have begun. With regard to my work, I should like to call the attention of beginning and intermediate students to the appendices listing courses in the language, history, and cultural heritage of Hungary that are available in the United States.

Hungarian Americans have been proud to live and work in the United States, which they find receptive and congenial to their heritage, values, and aims epitomized in the famous statement made by Louis Kossuth, the Hungarian statesman and expatriate, to the Ohio Legislature on February 6, 1852:

> The spirit of our age is democracy. -- All for the
> people, and all by the people. Nothing about the
> people without the people. -- That is democracy.
> And that is the ruling tendency of the spirit of our
> age.

Joseph Szeplaki
Wilson Library
University of Minnesota
Minneapolis, Minnesota

INDIVIDUAL IMMIGRATIONS (1583-1774)

Isolated arrivals of Hungarian immigrants are recorded through 1850, when there was a significant increase in their numbers as a result of the abortive Hungarian War of Independence.

According to the Chronicle of the Kings of Norway (Heimskringla), the crew of the Leif Ericsson expedition (ca.1000) included a man named Tyrker who, according to some scholars, may have been Hungarian. He "babbled in Turkish"; and, in Icelandic, "Tyrker" means "Turk." European records of the tenth century refer to Hungarians as "Turks." On the new shore, Tyrker found vines and grapes, and perhaps this prompted Ericsson to name the shore "Vineland" ("Wineland").

In 1507 Martin Waldseemüller (died 1512) published his Latin cosmography and named the American continent "America" in deference to the Christian name of the explorer Amerigo Vespucci. In a well-documented article published in Names (March, 1963), Zoltan J. Farkas amplifies the persuasive argument of Hungarian linguists that the Christian name of Vespucci derives ultimately from the name of the Hungarian eleventh-century saint, Emeric (Imre). Emeric was the son of St. Stephen, who reigned as the first Christian king of Hungary (1001-1038)

1583 The first undisputed Hungarian, Stephen Parmenius of Buda, a poet and humanist, arrived in America. He was employed by Sir Humphrey Gilbert as the official historian or chronicler of the colonizing voyage. Parmenius wrote in Latin and corresponded with Richard Hakluyt in England. He died at Cape Sable in a violent storm.

1680 John Ratkai, a Hungarian Jesuit, was assigned to New Mexico to do missionary work, where he fell victim to an Indian assault four years later.

1694 The translation of Increase Mather's De Successu Evangelii apud Indos Occidentales, in Nova Anglia etc. was published in Hungary. This was the first Hungarian book about America.

    John Kelp (Kelpio, Kelpius), born 1673 at Szasz-Dalya, Transylvania, Hungary, arrived in America via London. Kelp, who had studied theology in Hungary and Germany, became a hermit in Philadelphia, Pennsylvania. He died in 1708.

The district where he had lived was named "The Hermitage" and the street "The Hermit's Lane."

1695 — Isaac Ferdinand Sarossy, a man of colorful personality, arrived in Germantown near Philadelphia, Pennsylvania. It is probable that neither the primitive conditions of this colony nor the preacher's work without fixed compensation appealed to him. He left for Maryland two years later.

1759 — Father Ferdinand Konschak (or Konsag) died in California. Formerly a professor in Buda, he had left Hungary in the first part of the eighteenth century to become the head of the Mission of St. Ignotius in California and later visitator of all Californian missions.

THE AMERICAN REVOLUTION AND SUBSEQUENT YEARS (1776-1848)

1777 — One hundred forty-one Hungarians fought in the Revolution under the American flag. Since it was extremely difficult to obtain an officer's commission in the new American army, many additional Hungarians fought under the French flag in the auxiliary forces sent by France to aid the Americans in their struggle for independence.

January 13. Michael de Kovats, a Hungarian officer, offered his services to Benjamin Franklin in Paris, but Franklin declined his offer. Kovats then came to America and joined the Pulaski Legion, where he was appointed Colonel Commandant of the Legion on April 8, 1778. He helped in the organization of the cavalry which, even according to English opinion, was "the best cavalry the rebels ever had." Kovats died on the battlefield on May 11, 1779. His memorials can be seen at Charleston's Citadel, in Washington, D.C., and in New York.

1780 — Lauzun's Legion of Foreign Volunteers arrived on July 13, 1780, at Newport. The legion was part of the auxiliary forces sent by France under the treaty of alliance with the United States. One hundred forty hussars (cavalrymen) in Lauzun's legion were, in all probability, Hungarians. The records explicitly mention at least two Hungarians serving in Lauzun's legion. One is John Polereczky, a major of Lauzun's Polish lancers; the other is Francis Benyowsky, a lieutenant of Lauzun's hussars, who was the brother of the famous traveler and soldier of fortune, Count Mauritius Augustus Benyowsky. Francis Benyowsky died here in 1789.

1782   Count Mauritius Augustus Benyowsky, traveler and adventurer of legendary fame, presented a plan to General Washington about raising and transporting over three thousand foreign soldiers to serve the United States. Congress declined his offer. He left America but returned in 1784. His second expedition to the island of Madagascar was made possible with the financial help of several merchants in Baltimore.

1798   Several merchants from Hungary chose New Orleans for their new home. The first settler was Benjamin S. Spitzer, a Hungarian ship captain, who opened a large shop in town and sought to establish trade relations between the United States and Hungary.

1807   Maurice Fürst, a Hungarian-born engraver, settled in America and gained recognition.

1815   Alexander Farkas de Bölöni, a Hungarian traveler, met a few Hungarian Americans during his journey in the United States. He mentioned Francis Müller from Pozsony, whose uncle, Stephan Bock, had also come to America in 1815 and set up a fur trade in New Orleans.

1818   The Hungarian Gáspár Printz arrived in America in 1803. In his letter of January 7, 1818, he proudly described his new homeland as "a free country, without kings, ruled by presidents. Nobody is more noble than the other since all of us are nobles. Here people do not greet each other humbly, the poor is the same as the rich. Our country is a free republic. . . ."

1820   Mr. Schwatzer, born in Szekszard, Hungary, immigrated to the United States. He established the first Hungarian wine cellar in New York, becoming the initiator of Hungarian-American trade.

1829   Dr. Charles Luzenberg from Sopron, Hungary, came to New Orleans in 1829 and joined the medical staff of Charity Hospital. Subsequently, he became the founder and the first president of the New Orleans Medical Society.

1831   Alexander Farkas de Bölöni traveled during this year over most of America. Upon his return to Hungary, he published a book entitled Utazás Északamerikában (Journey in North America). He wrote both perceptively and sympathetically about the political, economic, and cultural conditions in the

United States. The book was influential in the Hungarian re-
form movement during an era of national revival. Bölöni,
together with two other Hungarian travelers, paid his respects to President Jackson. As far as we know, they were
the first Hungarians to be received in the White House.

1832   Charles Nagy, a well-known Hungarian mathematician and
astronomer, paid a visit to America. He established connections between the Hungarian Academy of Sciences and
the American Philosophical Society, founded by Benjamin
Franklin, and earned the friendship of President Jackson.
Nagy returned to Hungary but remained a great admirer of
the United States.

1833   Charles Krajtsir immigrated to America and became a
teacher of modern languages at the University of Virginia.

1836   The Hungarian nobleman Michael Eötvös settled in the United
States. He went back to Hungary in the wake of initial dis-
appointments but returned again with his family in 1854.

1837   Samuel Ludwigh, a Hungarian lawyer, arrived in America.
He lived in Baltimore and Philadelphia. Ludwigh switched
from law to journalism, becoming the editor of a German
newspaper in Philadelphia. In 1849, he wrote an article entitled "Hungary and Hungarian Sketches" for the New York
Tribune. A few years later he became publisher and editor
of an English-language periodical called The Torch.

1840   Augustus Haraszty, father of the California wine industry,
came to America as a traveler in 1840. He met the president at the White House and made the acquaintance of several prominent American figures including Daniel Webster.
He appeared at social events dressed in the resplendent at-
tire of a Hungarian nobleman and became the sensation of
Washington. Haraszty's life story made a fascinating read-
ing and entertainment for all. He was so impressed by
America that he returned in 1842 as a settler with his whole
family. In 1844, Haraszty's account of his American journey was published in Hungary and aroused considerable interest. It was a practical account of daily life in the United
States. Haraszty roamed all over the New Land. He founded
in Wisconsin the town of Haraszty, which is now Sauk City.
He tried his hand at different enterprises. He was a builder,
storekeeper, steamboat and ferry owner, leader of the Wisconsin Historical Society, etc. Eventually, he left for California in a covered wagon. In 1850, he arrived in San Diego,

where he became sheriff. He served in the legislature at Sacramento and was coin melter, refiner, and banker. He is best remembered for laying the foundations of the California wine industry. He established the first great wine planta- tions with grapevines imported from Hungary's great wine district of Tokay. His wines became popular in the United States under that name. He also wrote a valuable book en- titled Grape Culture, Wines and Wine making.

Attila Kelemen, a Hungarian tailor, made a fortune with his "miracle drug" called Tincturus Papricus, which was nothing but a mixture of paprika and whiskey. It was supposed to be extremely effective against cholera. His fame and wealth enabled him to obtain a job as a physician and to become the owner of a hospital and a pharmacy in New York.

FIRST WAVE: REFUGEES OF THE HUNGARIAN WAR OF
               INDEPENDENCE OF 1848-49

American Reaction and the First Arrivals

1848   March 15. The Hungarians revolted against Austria.

1849   May 28. Beginning this day, the New York Tribune pub-
              lished several articles dealing with a series of "Hungarian
              meetings" in New York. The first meeting was held in the
              Hotel Shakespeare on May 24, to celebrate the Hungarian
              victories in the Hungarian War of Independence. It was sug-
              gested at the meeting of May 31, that a confidential agent
              should be dispatched by the president to Hungary. Still later,
              after the defeat of Hungary, a demonstration against Austria
              and Russia was organized.

              June 18. Ambrose Dudley Mann was appointed by President
              Taylor to be a special and confidential agent of the United
              States to Hungary and authorized to recognize the revolu-
              tionary government of Hungary, but Austiran interference
              prevented him from reaching his destination.

              September. The Central Hungarian Society was formed in
              New York under the presidency of Gábor Naphegyi for the
              purpose of obtaining good will for Hungary in her struggle.
              It was the first Hungarian society in America.

              December 16. The first group of Hungarian refugees ar-
              rived in America. Most of them were cultured people of
              middle or upper class origin. Because of their humanistic

education, they lacked technical skills which were then in greatest demand in this country and were forced to work as laborers and farmhands. Their leader, László Ujházi, was Kossuth's representative in the United States before his visit. Ujházi was the first among the four thousand refugees to became a naturalized citizen. Twelve years later he was posted as consul in Italy by President Lincoln.

1850   Congress granted Ujházi and his group land in Iowa, where they started a Hungarian community named New Buda in Decatur County. Ujházi sought to organize the political life of the settlement after the American pattern and at the same time to preserve the Hungarian characteristics of social and domestic life. There were several other centers where Hungarians congregated in large numbers during the 1850s and 1860s. About thirty Hungarians made their home at New Orleans, Louisiana. A dozen or so chose St. Louis, Missouri, for their place of destiny. A few dozen Hungarians settled down at Davenport, Iowa.

KOSSUTH'S ARRIVAL

1851   President Fillmore was authorized by both the Senate and the House to send an American warship to Turkey to bring Louis Kossuth, the exiled Governor of Hungary, and his followers to the United States. Accordingly, Secretary of State Daniel Webster instructed the American Embassy in Turkey to embark Kossuth and his retinue, who then boarded the U.S.S. Mississippi.

September 7. On his way to America, Kossuth stopped over in England, while most of his followers went ahead aboard the Mississippi.

December 4. Following his men, Louis Kossuth arrived at Staten Island. He was invited to the White House and both Houses of Congress. On January 7, 1852, he spoke at the Legislative Banquet in Washington, D.C. Kossuth did not cross the ocean as an immigrant, but as a European statesman who had been invited to the United States. He was desirous of expressing his ideas, particularly about the "principle of intervention for non-intervention." His liberal political philosophy seemed to be far ahead of his time. His goal was to raise funds for an army so that he could resume the fight against Austria and to obtain the official support of the United States for this enterprise. He spoke to hundreds of American audiences, including legislative assemblies, during his tour. About two hundred and fifty poems, dozens of books, hundreds of pamphlets, and thousands of editorials were written in English about him during this period. His pro-Hungarian mission failed, but his impact on American society and his contribution to American social and political history were more extensive than is commonly realized.

Chronology of Louis Kossuth's Tour in 1851-52

1851   December 4. Arrived at Staten Island aboard the Humboldt.

            December 6. Arrived in New York City, where approximately 200,000 people greeted him.

            December 11. Corporation dinner at Irving House.

            December 15. Addressed the guests at the Press Banquet.

            December 16. Addressed the New York Militia.

            December 17. Meeting at Tammany Hall.

            December 18. Meeting at Plymouth Church, Brooklyn.

            December 19. Banquet at the Bar of New York.

            December 21. Addressed the Ladies of New York.

            December 23. Left New York for Philadelphia, where he spent the Christmas holidays.

            December 26. Left Philadelphia for Baltimore.

            December 30. Arrived at Washington, D.C.

            December 31. Visit at the White House.

1852   January 3. Dinner with President Fillmore.

            January 5. Reception in the Senate.

            January 7. Reception in the House. Legislative Banquet.

            January 12. Addressed the legislature at Annapolis, Maryland.

January 14-17. Harrisburg, Pennsylvania, Hollidaysburg, Pennsylvania.

January 21. Blairsville, Pennsylvania

January 22-31. Pittsburgh, Pennsylvania. Left for Cleveland and stopped on the way at Salem and Ravenna, Ohio.

February 4. Cleveland, Ohio.

February 6-7. Columbus, Ohio, where he addressed the legislature and met with Governor Wood.

February 9. On the way to Cincinnati he stopped at Xenia, Springfield, Dayton, and Hamilton, Ohio.

February 9-26. Cincinnati, Ohio. Enrolled in Lodge No. 133 of the Free and Accepted Masons.

February 26. Left Cincinnati for Madison, Ohio, by boat.

March 2. Indianapolis, Indiana, where he addressed the legislature.

March 3-7. Louisville, Kentucky. Left for St. Louis by boat.

March 9-16. St. Louis, Missouri. Left for New Orleans by boat.

March 21. Jackson, Mississippi, where he met Governor Foote.

March 26-31. New Orleans, Louisiana.

April 3. Mobile, Alabama.

April 5. Montgomery, Alabama.

April 7-9. LaGrange, Atlanta, Augusta, Georgia, and Charleston, South Carolina

April 10. Wilmington, North Carolina.

April 13. Washington, D.C., where he visited Mt. Vernon.

April 21. Trenton and Jersey City, New Jersey.

April 24. Newark, New Jersey. Left for New England on
a special train to Boston. On the way he stopped at Stam-
ford, Bridgeport, and New Haven, Connecticut; Springfield,
Chicopee, Holyoke, Whitneyville, and Northampton, Massachusetts.

April 26. Palmer, North Brookfield, Worcester, Westboro,
Framingham, Natick, Brookline, and Roxbury, Massachusetts.

April 27-30. Boston, Massachusetts, where he addressed
the legislature at Faneuil Hall.

May 3. Speech at Bunker Hill.

May 4. Cambridge, Massachusetts.

May 5. Lowell, Lynn, Salem, and Danvers, Massachusetts.

May 8. Boston, Massachusetts, where he addressed an audience of German immigrants.

May 10. Roxbury, Massachusetts.

May 11. West Cambridge, Lexington, and Concord, Massachusetts, where Ralph Waldo Emerson greeted him.

May 12. Plymouth, Massachusetts.

May 13. Fall River, Massachusetts.

May 14. Closing address in Boston, Massachusetts.

May 18. Pittsfield, Massachusetts. Arrived at Albany,
New York.

May 20. Speech at Albany, New York.

May 22. Buffalo and Niagara Falls, New York.

June 4. Syracuse, New York.

June 9. Utica, New York. Left for New York City, visiting
en route Schenectady and Troy, New York.

June 21. New York City, where he lectured in a Broadway Tabernacle.

June 23. Addressed a New York audience of German immigrants.

July 14. Sailed for England.

The Immigrants in the 1850s.

1850-51 A Hungarian Club was founded in Boston by George L. Stearns, an admirer of Louis Kossuth and a sympathizer with the Hungarian War of Independence. Many Hungarian immigrants visited his house, among them Edward Zerdahelyi, the famous Hungarian concert pianist.

1851 Mátyás Nyujtó arrived in New York as an immigrant and in a short time opened the first Hungarian restaurant and saloon, To the Three Hungarians.

August 13. Captain John Prágay, whose book dealing with the Hungarian War of Independence was the first on the subject to be translated into English, committed suicide to escape execution in Cuba. He participated with eight other Hungarians in the ill-fated revolutionary expedition of Narisco Lopez.

While traveling in Hungary, the American clergyman and philanthropist Charles Loring Brace was arrested by Austrian authorities on the charge of conspiring against the state with exiled Hungarians. He was eventually released from custody upon the protest of the United States government. Returning to America, he wrote a book about his experiences and aroused considerable popular sentiment against Austria.

1852 One hundred thirteen Hungarians residing in New York City drafted and signed a statement expressing their loyalty to Kossuth and defending him against Austrian charges of malfeasance which had appeared in the American press. Approximately two to three hundred Hungarians may have lived in the city during this decade.

Kossuth's two sisters, Susanne and Emilia, arrived in New York. Both died in America, Susanne in 1854 and Emilia in 1860.

A Hungarian Revolutionary conspiracy was discovered by
the Austrian secret police in Transylvania, Hungary. Its
members were executed, but the three secret agents of Kossuth -- Mátyás Rózsafy, József Makk, and Fülöp Figyelmessy -- escaped and came to the United States.

The short-lived Hungarian Sick and Benefit Society was
founded by Philip Freund and Charles Kornis in New York
for the purpose of aiding Hungarian immigrants.

1853   Martin Koszta, a Hungarian immigrant and resident in the
United States, was visiting Turkey, where he was kidnapped
and detained on an Austrian warship in the harbor of Smyrna
as an Austrian subject of Hungarian nationality. Upon instructions of the American government, Com. D.N. Ingraham, captain of the U.S. sloop of war St. Louis, delivered on July 2 an ultimatum to Captain von Schwarz,
commander of the Austrian brig of war Hussar, and succeeded in obtaining the release of the kidnapped Hungarian
American. In pressing for this release, Secretary of State
William Marcy argued that Koszta, though not a naturalized
citizen, had been granted resident status and was therefore
entitled to the protection of the United States. The legal
principle articulated by Marcy in the response of the American government to this international incident set a precedent.
Subsequently, President Pierce stated that "the United States
would adhere to the same principle in the future." The incident known as the Koszta Affair was widely and fully reported in the American press and is still taught in courses
dealing with American diplomatic history and with the American construction of international law.

August 23. Lázár Mészáros, Minister of War and Commander
in Chief of the Hungarian Army in 1848-49, arrived in New
York. He bought a farm of 23 acres at Scotch Plain, New
Jersey, and became the first Hungarian farmer in that state.

The first Hungarian newspaper, Száműzöttek Lapja (Journal
of Hungarian Exiles) was published in New York by Charles
Kornis. It served cultural and propaganda purposes for the
followers of Kossuth. Six issues were printed.

1854   Bernát Bettelheim, Hungarian missionary and medical doctor living on the Japanese island of Ryukyu, served as an
interpreter for Commodore Perry and left for America in
one of his "black ships." In 1926, a statue of Bettelheim
was erected on Ryukyu.

1856   Ignace Hainer, a Hungarian refugee and settler at New Buda
              in Iowa, became a professor of modern languages at the
              University of Columbia, Missouri. He held that position for
              four years, when he was dismissed together with other pro-
              fessors for his anti-slavery stand.

              The Hungarian scientist and explorer John Xantus, as a mem-
              ber of the United States Survey Expedition commissioned to
              explore Kansas Territory, led his team of twenty-nine men
              into Southern Kansas and reached the source of the Arkansas
              River. They returned with a large collection of natural sci-
              ence materials which were given to the Smithsonian Institu-
              tion. Xantus was made a member of the Academy of Natural
              Sciences, the American Philosophical Society in Philadelphia,
              and the Atheneum in Boston.

1857   The United States Department of Interior appointed John
              Xantus leader of the United States Coast Survey. He estab-
              lished his headquarters in Southern California, and took his
              team into the Mojave Desert, the San Bernardino Valley,
              and Sierra Nevada Country.

1858   Michael Heilprin, a former writer in Hungary and an active
              member in the New York Hungarian society, began his work
              for Appleton's New American Encyclopedia, editing and
              writing a large number of articles.

1859   Daniel Fiske included in his book published on the occasion
              of the American Chess Congress a letter by Jakab Janos
              Löwenthal, the great Hungarian chessmaster, which de-
              scribed Löwenthal's escape and arrival in the United States.
              Löwenthal is best remembered by historians of American
              chess as the opponent, friend, and supporter in both England
              and the United States of Paul Morphy, the prodigy from
              Louisiana, who -- in his brief and meteoric career -- van-
              quished the strongest chessmasters in both the Old and the
              New World.

                              The Civil War

1860   Julian Kune, a naturalized Hungarian immigrant, attended,
              as an alternate delegate, the Republican Convention that
              nominated Lincoln as candidate for president. After the
              convention, Kune campaigned for Lincoln in Indiana, deli-
              vering speeches in both English and German. He had meet-
              ings with Lincoln on different occasions. Kune served in the

Civil War as major in the 24th Illinois Volunteer Infantry
Regiment and later wrote an autobiography.

1861   Michael Heilprin started to work for the Nation in Washington, writing articles on European politics for over twenty
years.

Joseph Czapkay came to America via Turkey. He had been
a barber in Hungary but presented himself as a doctor and
became quite wealthy in California. He was named United
States ambassador to Bucharest, Rumania, in about 1861.

Not many Hungarian immigrants settled in the Confederate
States, with the exception of Missouri, because they de-
tested slavery. That might explain why only one Hungarian
is known to have held a commission in the Confederate Army.
He was B. Estv́an, a cavalry colonel. Even he left the service after a short period of time. Since many of the immigrants had fought for the liberation of the Hungarian serfs,
and were ex-revolutionaries, about 800 (20 percent) of the
4000 Hungarians living in America joined the Union forces.
(This degree of participation exceeds that of any other ethnic group in America.) Among the 800 Hungarians serving
under the Union flag, there were 2 major generals, 5 brigadier generals, 15 colonels, 2 lieutenants colonels, 14 ma-
jors, 15 captains, and a number of subalterns and surgeons.

The personality of Gen. John C. Fremont attracted Hungarians. There were about two dozen Hungarian officers in
Fremont's Western army. They played a prominent role in
the Missouri, Kansas, Illinois, and Kentucky campaigns.

At the age of seventeen, Nicholas Fej́erv́ary, Jr., the only
son of Nicholas Fej́erv́ary, the Hungarian immigrant and
benefactor of the city of Davenport, Iowa, enlisted under the
Union flag and was killed in one of the early battles. He was
the first recorded second-generation Hungarian-American
to give his life for the United States. The following Union
soldiers were all first-generation Hungarian immigrants,
most of whom had fought in the Hungarian War of Independence.

John T.A. Fiala, the distinguished topographical engineer
and compiler of the first large scale map of Missouri, served
as lieutenant colonel of the St. Louis National Guard. Later
he was on the staff of Gen. John C. Fremont as colonel. Fiala designed and supervised the fortification of St. Louis.

One of the first Hungarian volunteers, Geza Mihalotzy, organized the Chicago Lincoln Riflemen composed of Hungarians and Bohemians. Special permission was given by President Lincoln to name the unit in his honor. When the company merged with the 24th Illinois Infantry Regiment, Mihalotzy became colonel of the regiment. He died in 1864 of a war injury at Chattanooga, Tennessee. Fort Mihalotzy on Fameron Hill was named in his honor.

May 23. George Utassy organized the New York Garibaldi Guard, part of the 39th New York Infantry Regiment. He became the first colonel of this unit. A Hungarian flag was presented to it in addition to the American and Garibaldi flags, since half of the men in the Garibaldi Guard had been born in Hungary.

October 25. Major Charles Zagonyi's "death-ride" routed the Confederates and cleared the nearby town of Springfield, Missouri, of the enemies, thus saving Missouri, claimed by both sides, for the Union. General Fremont had commissioned Zagonyi to organize and command a cavalry unit which became known as Fremont's Body Guard.

The former Hungarian hussar officer selected the horses for the cavalry personally and designed its dashing uniforms. The "death-ride" was a cavalry charge led by Zagonyi against 2000 Confederate soldiers defending a hill at Springfield. Upon learning that the defending force was nearly seven times larger than he had been led to believe, Fremont wanted to cancel the attack but was persuaded by Zagonyi to permit it against overwhelming odds. The result is described in the inscription on the granite monument at Springfield as one of "the most daring and brilliant cavalry charges of the Civil War." Zágonyi has been celebrated in poems, paintings, and stories for his heroic activities.

Albert Anzelm was named lieutenant colonel of the 3rd Missouri Infantry Regiment. Later he was promoted to colonel and became General Fremont's chief of staff. Anzelm was severely wounded in the Battle of Wilson Creek.

Hailed by Giuseppe Garibaldi as "the hero of heroes" for his bravery in Italy, Fülöp Figyelmessi came to America in 1861, and served as American consul in British Guinea for more than twenty years. He served in the Civil War under General Fremont and was appointed inspector general at Wheeling, West Virginia.

For his active part in the organization of the 10th Iowa Volunteer Regiment, Nicholas Perczel was named its first colonel. The regiment went into battle in early 1862. It was part of the army that captured 5,000 Confederate soldiers near Tipton, Missouri. This regiment participated also in the siege of Corinth. The battle near Iuka, Missouri, resulted in heavy losses for the regiment. Brigadier generals Schuyler Hamilton and John C. Sullivan had high praise for Colonel Perczel's brave conduct in the service.

1862   Alexander Jekelfalussy, while serving as a lieutenant in the 24th Illinois Regiment, submitted his resignation to the commanding officer of the regiment, Géza Mihalótzy. Jekelfalussy stated that his resignation was prompted by his conscientious objection to the standing order requiring each regiment to give up fugitive slaves hiding in its camp. His resignation was not accepted.

Gabriel Korponay was appointed lieutenant colonel of the 28th Pennsylvania Volunteer Infantry Regiment. The famous polka dancer Korponay had come to America around 1840. He served as captain in the 3rd Missouri Volunteer Cavalry Regiment and participated in the Mexican War. He taught fencing at a small private boys' school in St. Louis. Brig. Gen. George Dashiel Bayard, killed in action at Fredericksburg, Virginia, had been one of his students. Korponay left for Hungary to fight in the War of Independence of 1848-49, but Hungarian resistance had already been crushed by the Russian and Austrian armies by the time he arrived. Korponay returned to America and worked as an interpreter for the Eastern District of the U.S. Court. In 1858, he wrote a letter to Attorney General J.J. Crittenden and offered his services and those of a hundred other volunteers in the upcoming struggle.

Frederich Knefler was appointed colonel of the 79th Indiana Volunteer Regiment. Previously, he had served as adjutant to Gen. Lew Wallace, author of the famous Biblical novel Ben Hur. Colonel Knefler commanded a brigade in the division of General Wood in the battles of Nashville, Chattanooga, and Franklin, Tennessee. He was also in command of the 86th Indiana Regiment in the battle of Missionary Ridge. At the end of the war, he was appointed brigadier general. After the war, President Hayes appointed him chief of the Pension Office. Later he became a member of a committee for erecting memorials to heroes of the Civil War.

The 22nd Volunteer Infantry Regiment of New Jersey was organized by Cornelius Fornet, who also became its first colonel. Before his appointment, he had served under General Fremont as major of engineers.

1863   Anthony Vallas, who had settled at New Orleans and eventually became president of the New Orleans Academy of Sciences, lost his job as professor of mathematics and natural philosophy at the Seminary of Learning of the State of Louisiana (Louisiana State University) because of pro-Union sympathies.

Peter Paul Dobozy enlisted in the 2nd Tennessee Heavy Artillery Regiment. In the same year he became adjutant to General Asboth and commander of the 4th Colored Heavy Artillery Regiment at Fort Columbus, Kentucky. Dobozy had organized the above-mentioned regiment.

Julius Stahel-Szamvald helped to organize the 8th New York Volunteer Infantry Regiment and became its first lieutenant colonel. His regiment protected the rear of the Union Army as it retreated after the defeat at Bull Run. Stahel-Szamwald participated bravely in many of the early battles and was promoted to brigadier in 1861 and to major general two years later. In March 1863, he was appointed commander of the cavalry defending Washington, at the personal request of President Lincoln. For his bravery in the battle of Piedmont in 1864 he received the Congressional Medal of Honor in 1893. From November 1864 to January 1865, while recuperating from his war wounds, he served as president of the military court in Baltimore. Stahel-Szamwald continued to serve the country in peaceful times. He was in the foreign service of the United States for eleven years as American consul in Japan and China.

Three sons of Emilia Kossuth served the United States with distinction. After commanding the 51st Colored Regiment, Ladislaus Zsulavsky organized the 82nd U.S. Colored Infantry Regiment and became its colonel. He also fought with General Asboth in the division of Maj. Gen. Gordon Granger as commander of the first brigade of the District of West Florida, which included the 25th, 82nd, and 86th Colored Infantry Regiments. His two brothers, Sigismund and Emil, were both lieutenants in the 82nd Colored Regiment. Sigismund died of typhoid fever in 1863.

1864   Eugene Kozlay enlisted in the 54th New York Volunteer Infantry Regiment (The Black Jaegers) and became its colonel. In view of his meritorious services, Kozlay was appointed brigadier general in 1865.

1865   One of the four brothers Rombauer, Raphael G., served as major of artillery in the West Tennessee District. In 1865, he became commander of the entire artillery unit of that dis-district. Robert J. Rombauer was colonel of the 1st Missouri Volunteer Infantry Regiment U.S. Reserve Corps. Later he became commander of the 2nd brigade of the Army of the Southwest. He was also a Civil War historian. Roland Rombauer was captain in the 1st Florida Cavalry in the District of West Florida under the command of General Asbóth. Later he was promoted to provost marshal. Roderick Rombauer served as judge of the Circuit Court and became one of the best known jurists in the State of Missouri. As captain he served in the 1st Regiment of the U.S. Reserve. The town of Rombauer was named after him.

Charles Mundee-Mándy was promoted to brigadier general for his bravery in the battle of Petersburg, Virginia. He fought in the battles of Winchester, Fisher Hill, and Cedar Creek, Virginia. He was wounded at Cedar Creek as well as in the battle at Spotsylvania Court House, Virginia.

October 14. The first significant immigrant institution, the New York Hungarian Association (New Yorki Magyar Egylet) was formed for the purpose of nourishing the fraternal spirit among its members and awakening sympathy for Hungary, studying American institutions to popularize them in Hungary, and stimulating the scientific and mercantile work of Hungarians in the United States. The first president of the Association was Colonel Perczel and its leading spirit Michael Heilprin. Several years later the association branched into a choral society and in 1871 into a Sickness Benefit Society. The last public undertaking of the association was the reception of the Hungarian delegates to the St. Louis Interparliamentary Congress in 1904.

1866   Theodore Majthényi was appointed lieutenant of the 6th U.S. Cavalry. As lieutenant and adjutant to the Cavalry Guard under the command of Zágonyi, Majthényi participated in the famous charge at Springfield.

George Pomutz, the United States consul at St. Petersburg, Russia, also fought in the Civil War. He took part in the organization of the 15th Iowa Volunteer Infantry Regiment and was promoted to lieutenant colonel. He became commander of the Third Brigade under General Sherman in the Army of Tennessee. While in the 15th Iowa Regiment, Pomutz took part in several battles.

President Grant appointed Alexander Asboth United States minister to the Argentine Republic for his valuable services in the Civil War. Asboth, who had been adjutant to Kossuth during the War of 1848-49, had accompanied him into exile and on his American tour. After Kossuth's departure, Asboth remained in the United States. He is credited with the planning of Central Park in New York. Immediately after the outbreak of the Civil War, Asbóth enlisted and became the chief of staff of Gen. John C. Fremont in 1861. He was appointed brigadier general in the same year. He took part in the Southern Missouri Campaign. Camp Asboth was named after him. He was wounded in the battle of Pear Ridge, Arkansas. After the Missouri Campaign, he was given command of the West Florida Department. The wounds affected his subsequenty health and contributed to his early death. In spite of his deteriorating health, he performed his diplomatic duties with distinction.

1867   A compromise (in German "Ausgleich" meaning "equalization") was signed by Hungary and Austria. Hungary was granted autonomy and self-government within the framework of the dual monarchy. A number of Hungarian refugees returned to their native land to take advantage of the political amnesty following the compromise.

1869   The first Hungarian-language play was presented in New York by amateurs on Horeston Street.

Second Wave: Economic Immigration (1870-1917)

1870   Rapid industrial expansion in the United States created such a shortage of laborers that desperate measures were taken to induce the poor people of Europe to come here. Large corporations sent representatives into Hungary at the end of the nineteenth century to recruit workers. These agents did not always abide by immigration laws, and many abuses were recorded. From 1870 onward there was a mass emigration from Hungary to the United States. Since full-scale industrialization had not yet reached Hungary, the emigrants escaped from the poverty and the misery of the Hungarian semi-feudal system. They were, for the most part, unskilled agrarian laborers who left their native country for economic rather than ideological reasons. Many came to the United States with the intention of saving money and returning to Hungary to live there in better material circumstances. Broken families, men outnumbering women, shocking congestions, and unpleasant living and working conditions characterized the life of most immigrants round the turn of the century. Their departure confronted the government of Hungary with a dilemma. On the one hand, it was better for the dissatisfied to leave than to stay and riot; on the other hand, entire villages became depopulated. From 1900 onward, the Hungarian government tried to improve living and working conditions at home in order to reduce the number of economic emigrants. At the same time, it tried to lure the moneyed American Hungarians back to Hungary by strengthening their ties with their native land, e.g. by sending them free flags and books, subsidizing Hungarian language newspapers in America, and sending ministers to serve their congregations. At the outbreak of World War I, most immigrants abandoned the idea of returning home. They had settled mostly near the mines and steel furnaces of Ohio, Pennsylvania, New York, and New Jersey. However, large groups had also settled in Illinois, Indiana, and West Virginia.

It is difficult to estimate the number of Hungarian immigrants during this period. The Ninth Census of the United States in 1870 distinguishes Hungarians from Austrians, but it classifies as Hungarians the members of ethnic minorities (e.g., Czechs, Slovaks, Ruthenians, Rumanians, Serbians, and Croatians) who were born within the boundaries of Hungary as a self-governing kingdom within the framework of the dual monarchy from 1867 to 1918. The American census has traditionally designated the nationality of immigrants according to whatever independent country they happen to have been born in. Many of the immigrants, however, have understandably designated their nationality according to what they consider their native tongue. (It might also be noted that, following 1918, many native Hungarians born in newly created and expanded states neighboring Hungary were classified by the American census and Western history books as non-Hungarians.) This explains the difference between the immigration figures and the figures of Americans of Hungarian origin. Between 1870 and 1920 the

approximate number of immigrants from Hungary was
1,998,199. About 54.5 percent declared Hungarian as their
native tongue. The rest belonged to other nationalities. That
makes the approximate number of self-professed Hungarians
somewhat over one million. In 1920, Hungarians constituted
about 1 percent of the total U.S. population.

1871   Michael Heilprin was chosen editor and put in charge of the
second edition of the American Encyclopedia for five years.

1874   March. Dr. Árpád Gerster, the famous surgeon, arrived
in America. He was elected president of the New York Medical Society in 1891 and in the same year given membership in the Budapest Medical Association in recognition for
his work. Gerster became professor of surgery at Columbia University in 1910, and in the following year he was
elected president of the American Medical Association.

1881   The Hungarian government tried to regulate emigration and
forbade agencies to operate without a license. Emigrants
were permitted to leave Hungary only on accredited liners.
The first Hungarian emigration law was ineffective since
it was not strictly enforced.

1882   James Kovács, representative of the Hungarian Unitarian
Church in the Saratoga Unitarian Conference, toured the
large cities in the United States, speaking about Hungarians
and the Hungarian Unitarian Church before university and
Sunday audiences. He spent five months on this tour.

1884   The first Hungarian Folk Festival was held in New York with
a parade through the Hungarian district of Houston Street
and Avenue B to Sulzer's Harlem River Park. Contests,
games, speeches, and the display of folk costumes were included in the activities of the day-long festival. The Folk
Festival became an annual event, and its revenue was used
to fund the Hungarian Association of New York. The festival
was duplicated in other cities, too.

New York's first Hungarian Conversational and Sickness
Aid Association was founded in 1884. It propagated the Hungarian language in addition to providing benefits.

February 1. A bimonthly journal, the American National
Guard (Amerikai Nemzetör) was published in New York. It
united the Hungarians scattered in the United States. It was

the only Hungarian-language newspaper until the Szabadság (Liberty) was founded. The guiding spirit of the newspaper was Gusztáv Sz. Erdélyi, for whom many journalists of the later Hungarian American Press worked.

1885   The Hungarian Association (Magyar Társulat) was organized in New York under the presidency of the famous Hungarian surgeon Dr. Árpád Gerster for the purpose of aiding the Hungarian immigrants arriving in New York. It supplied legal advice, provided money and clothes for the needy, bought return tickets for destitute immigrants desirous of going back to Hungary, sent a guide to the port of entry in America, and specialized in the transfer of funds. It also operated a travel bureau. The Association was dissolved in 1896 as a result of financial difficulties.

A number of Hungarian American fraternal insurance companies came into existence after the tidal wave of Hungarian mass immigration had reached America. One of the largest, oldest, and most important organizations, the Verhovay Fraternal Insurance Association (Verhovay Segély Egylet), was founded at Hazleton, Pennsylvania in 1886. At its first public meeting in 1887, the Association possessed $86.18. It began to make fast progress in 1909. By 1926, the Association had $1,636,054.00. Eventually, it became one of the big four Hungarian-American insurance agencies. The Verhovay association is said to have been organized by Hungarian miners after a sick Hungarian roomer had been thrown out into the street for inability to pay his rent. The Hungarian immigrants joined the Hungarian associations rather than the American labor unions because the former gave wider coverage and their native tongue was spoken there. Aside from providing indispensable insurance, the Hungarian associations became centers of social life. They were characterized by strong national sentiment.

November 15. Mihály Munkácsy, the world-famous Hungarian painter, arrived in New York. His monumental painting "Christ before Pilate" was shown to the representatives of the press on November 17. The exhibition was a tremendous success, and the painting was bought by John Wanamaker, who kept it on display in his store in Philadelphia. Munkacsy returned to Europe, but left behind great works of art in museums, libraries, and private collections. His celebrated painting of the blind Milton dictating his poetry to his daughters is still displayed at the New York Public Library.

1887   A health benefit and funeral association, The Count Batthy-
            any Association, was founded in Cleveland, Ohio. It was
            Named after the martyred Hungarian Premier of 1848, whose
            fate struck a sympathetic chord in the breast of Hungarian
            immigrants.

1888   January. József Black immigrated to America in 1857. He
            settled in Cleveland in 1873. President Grover Cleveland
            appointed him United States consul in Budapest, Hungary,
            in 1888.

1889   The first Hungarian literary society was formed in New
            York.

1891   The Hungarian-language newspaper Szabadság (Liberty)
            was founded in Cleveland. Starting as a weekly, it developed
            into the first full-fledged Hungarian American daily news-
            paper. Its founder was Tihamér Kohányi. President Taft at-
            tended the celebration of the twentieth anniversary of the
            newspaper.

1892   The first Hungarian Catholic parish was started by Charles
            Bohn in Cleveland, Ohio. In 1894, he also founded the week-
            ly Catholic Hungarians' Sunday, which is still published to-
            day.

            The Federation of Hungarian Fraternal Societies (Magyar
            Betegsegélyző Egyletek Szövetsége) was founded in Bridge-
            port, Connecticut, attempting to unite all Hungarian Ameri-
            can fraternal societies. A convention of the Federation was
            held in Philadelphia, Pennsylvania, but the delegates could
            not agree on a common goal. The Federation expired two
            years later, and small fraternal organizations mushroomed.

            In the midwest, a fraternal association (the Baross Gábor
            Association) was founded in St. Paul, Minnesota. The asso-
            ciation existed until 1973.

            September. Hungarians in America organized festivities
            for the ninetieth anniversary of Kossuth's birthday.

1893   The Fejérvári Home for the aged was opened at Davenport,
            Iowa. It was the gift of a successful Hungarian real-estate
            man of the city, Nicholas Fejérvári, who also bequeathed
            his large garden to the public. It was named Fejérvári Park
            in his honor.

1896   Hungary celebrated her millenium as a nation. Hungarian
            millenary festivities were held all over America to com-
            memorate the 1000 years of the existence of Hungary as a
            state. The most important ones were at Pittsburgh, Penn-
            sylvania; McKeesport, Pennsylvania; San Francisco, Cali-
            fornia; Buda, Georgia; Bridgeport, Connecticut; and Cleve-
            land, Ohio.

            June 18. The delegation of the Cleveland Hungarians left
            New York for Budapest in order to take part in the millenary
            festivities. This was the first time that the Hungarian -
            Americans were officially and cordially received in Hun-
            gary.

1897   The decision had been made in Cleveland to establish the
            fraternal organization of the Hungarian Protestants, named
            the Hungarian Reformed Federation of America (Amerikai
            Magyar Reformatus Egyesület). It gave life and health pro-
            tection to its members and developed into one of the Big
            Four Hungarian fraternal bodies. Since many of its mem-
            bers considered their stay in America temporary, they took
            active interest in the constitutional struggle that was taking
            place in Hungary. The Federation's most efficacious means
            of putting pressure on the Hungarian government was the re-
            fusal to transmit insurance payments falling due in that
            country. In 1972, the Federation had 30,309 members, and
            its assets were $17,049,213.48.

1902   September 1. A great reception was organized in New York
            to celebrate the arrival of the elaborate Hungarian banner
            sent by the Hungarian National Society to Hungarian-Ameri-
            cans. It was a gesture of appreciation for the money given
            by Hungarian-Americans for the erection of the statue of the
            poet Vörösmarty in Budapest. The banner was rotated among
            various Hungarian associations and transferred annually
            from one association to another within the framework of a
            dignified ceremony.

            September 27. The unveiling of the Kossuth statue in Cleve-
            land took place as an expression of the high esteem in which
            Hungarians in America held Kossuth. The bronze statue
            was the copy of the Kossuth statue in Nagy Szalonta, Hungary.
            It was erected on University Circle in Cleveland. The gov-
            ernor of Ohio, Mr. Nash, spoke at the unveiling ceremonies.
            Famous social and political personages were also present.

1903   In Hungary a law was enacted to regulate all agencies deal-
               ing with the transportation of emigrants. Henceforth, these
               agencies had to obtain licenses from the Hungarian Minis-
               try of the Interior.

1904   The Hungarian government signed an agreement with the
               Cunard Line. In exchange for the monopoly on the transpor-
               tation of Hungarian immigrants to America, Cunard pledged
               to establish a line between Fiume and New York and to op-
               erate it within the limits of Hungarian emigration laws.

1906   Edward Zerdahelyi, a distinguished pianist, died in German-
               town, Pennsylvania. He had been one of the pupils and
               friends of Franz Liszt. In 1849, he had escaped to America.
               He was one of the members of Stearns' Hungarian Club and
               served in the Garibaldi Guard of New York during the Civil
               War. He spent the last twenty years of his life in Philadel-
               phia as professor of music at the Sacred Heart Convent
               (Eden Hall, Torresdale).

               September 16. The Washington statue sent by Hungarian-
               Americans was unveiled in Budapest. The idea of sending
               the statue was that of Tihamér Koháyni, who had a great
               share in its realization.

               The American Hungarian Federation in Washington, D.C.,
               an association of societies, institutes, and churches, was
               established to defend the interests of Americans of Hungar-
               ian origin in the United States.

               The American Hungarian People's Voice started a campaign
               to save Henric Demar, a Hungarian immigrant who had been
               unjustly accused of murder in Nevada. The newspaper
               turned to the Hungarian-American public for help. By Janu-
               ary 22, 1908, enough money had been collected to hire a
               well-known defense lawyer, who managed to secure Demar's
               acquittal.

1907   This was the peak year of Hungarian immigration; altogether
               60,071 immigrants were admitted to the country in the
               course of twelve months.

               Angelo Heilprin, famous geologist and professor and the
               son of Michael Heilprin, died. He had been president of the
               American Earth Study Society and the American Geographi-
               cal Society. He had also participated in the Peary expedi-
               tion to Greenland.

1909   The first Hungarian engineers' and architects' association
            was formed in New York.

1910   According to Géza Hoffman's data, in 1910 there were 1,046
            Hungarian charitable and health insurance societies in the
            United States. The total number of Hungarian associations
            in the same year was 1,600.

1911   Count Albert Apponyi, the noted Hungarian diplomat and
            statesman, visted the United States. He spoke on the sub-
            ject of peace to both Houses of Congress as well as to Hun-
            garian-Americans.

1912   Joseph Pulitzer, a Hungarian immigrant and the founder of
            modern journalism, left a two and one-half million dollar
            fund for the establishment of the School of Journalism at
            Columbia University in 1912. The Columbia University
            trustees have continued to award the famous prizes in jour-
            nalism and literature he established. Joseph Pulitzer was
            born in Makó, Hungary, in 1847. He came to America in
            1864 and participated in the Civil War. The young veteran
            lived as a hobo, then became a reporter on the Westliche
            Post, St. Louis. Having studied law, he was admitted to
            the bar in 1868. Soon he became part owner of the West-
            liche Post. In 1869, Pulitzer served as a member of the
            Missouri Legislature. In 1874, he participated in the State
            Constitutional Convention in Missouri. In 1876, he was
            elected congressman from Missouri. He aligned himself
            with the reform movement. He also bought the St. Louis
            Dispatch and merged it with the Westliche Post to form the
            Post-Dispatch. In 1883, Pulitzer became the owner and pub-
            lisher of the New York World, which rapidly achieved mass
            popularity. The end of his life was marred by blindness.

            Louis Heilprin, second son of Michael Heilprin, died. He
            had edited the New International Encyclopedia and the litera-
            ture section for the Evening Post.

1913   Ayer's American Newspaper Annual and Directory listed
            sixteen Hungarian-language papers in the United States, but
            the figure does not include the papers published after the
            turn of the century by many Hungarian settlements for their
            own exclusive use. In any case, the increasing number of
            newspapers reflected the great wave of recent Hungarian
            immigrants and their growing demand for such publications.
            Eventually, the newspapers were consolidated; and, since

there was no competition, the Hungarian-American press did not, on the whole, become a truly progressive organ of education and public opinion during the pre-war and the war period.

Third Wave: Political Refugees (1918-1974)

The fifty-six years following 1918 constitute one of the most tragic periods in the overall history of Hungary. The geographic boundaries, as well as the social, economic and political developments, were continually changing and shifting during this period. The transformation into a socialist republic followed by the Bolshevist Revolution of 1919 and then by the restoration of an independent Hungarian monarchy, the Peace Treaty of Trianon, the pressures and policies es of Nazi Germany, Hungarian participation in the Second World War, the sub sequent Soviet Russian occupation and the development of a socialist Communist state, and -- last but not least -- the abortive revolution of 1956 uprooted huge masses of native Hungarians. The shifting and often contradictory ideological and political orientations induced thousands and later tens of thousands to emigrate from Hungary. These emigrants may be classified as political refugees, though many of them were also prompted to leave for concomitant economic reasons.

This large-scale emigration has had a far-ranging effect on the life of Hungarian-Americans. It revivified and rejuvenated their sense of community which had been in danger of weakening and disappearing altogether. And, of course, it made significant contributions to American society and history, too.

After the First World War

1920   The first American Hungarian anthology was compiled by Ernest Rickert, a Catholic priest. It was entitled American Hungarian Poets and published in Budapest. The compiler was the first scholar of American Hungarian literature.

June 4. The Peace Treaty of Trianon, concluding Hungary's participation in the First World War as a member of the Austro-Hungarian dual monarchy, was signed in France. According to the provisions of the treaty, Hungary became an independent state but lost approximately two-thirds of her pre-1918 territory (232,448 out of 325,411 square kilometers) and approximately half of her pre-1918 population

(10,050,575 out of 20,886,487). The lost territories and people were attached to existing, sometimes newly created, neighboring states. The majority of people living in most of these lost territories were non-Hungarian ethnic minorities so that the territories were claimed by the adjacent states on the basis of the self-determination of their inhabitants. In any case, of the 10,050,515 people living in the lost territories, 3,219,579 claimed Hungarian to be their native tongue. And, regardless of the justice or injustice of these territorial settlements, the political, economic, and social impact of the overnight reduction of land and population was tremendous. For example, most of Hungary's natural resources and much of her heavy industry happened to be located in the lost territories. As a result, the newly reduced country was soon in the throes of recession, inflation, and unemployment aggravated by the flight to the mother country of tens of thousands of Hungarians who did not wish to live under foreign rule in neighboring countries. Many of the Hungarians who suddenly found themselves living "abroad" emigrated to the United States.

1921   During a period of fourteen years ending on June 30, 1921, sixty-seven percent of the Hungarian immigrants returned from the United States to Hungary.

1922   A department of Hungarian was established at Franklin and Marshall College at Lancaster, Pennsylvania. Twenty-five students were enrolled annually in classes offered by the department over the next fourteen years.

1923   Albert Béla Alexay received the first of three Gold Medals awarded to him by the Charles Coffin Foundation.

1926   The first Hungarian physicians' society was founded in New York.

1927   The first history of Hungarian-Americans was published in Hungarian by the Szabadság newspaper in Cleveland. Written by Geza Kende, it was entitled Magyarok Amerikában, Az amerikai magyarság története 1583-1927 (Hungarians in America: The History of Hungarians in America, 1583-1927). Kende's two-volume, 874-page book deserves much credit for his painstaking original research.

1928   March 15. Hungarians in New York erected a bronze statue of Kossuth on Riverside Drive. The memorial was unveiled in the presence of a delegation from the Hungarian Parliament. Géza D. Berkó, editor of the largest American Hungarian-language newspaper, Amerikai Magyar Nepszava (American Hungarian People's Voice), had spearheaded the drive for funds.

1929   August 22-24. The first International Congress of Hungarians was held in Hungary. The avowed aim of the Congress was to try to unite the Hungarians scattered throughout the world. This seemed to be the first official recognition in Hungary proper of a Hungarian diaspora as well as of the immense energies and potentialities inherent in it. Fifty-two Hungarian American organizations sent 125 delegates to represent them at this Congress.

The American Hungarian Federation held a national meeting in Buffalo and discussed extensively the dismemberment of Hungary and the aims of reunification. Previously there were two other meetings held in Cleveland and devoted to the same subject.

1930   Charles Feleky, the Hungarian-born American musician, book collector, researcher, and the manager of the Martin Beck Theater, died this year. He was the first scholarly researcher of Hungarian materials in the United States. His library consisted of more than 10,000 magazine articles and over 6,000 volumes. Feleky also spent twenty-five years in compiling a bibliography of all works pertaining to Hungary and Hungarians. In 1930, the bibliography consisted of nineteen manuscript volumes. Unfortunately, his valuable collection was distributed among American libraries, and the bibliography was lost. Only the catalogue of his library was microfilmed by the Library of Congress.

1931   July 15-16. An airplane named "Justice for Hungary" crossed the Atlantic Ocean, piloted by two Hungarians (George Endrész and Alexander Magyar), to protest the Treaty of Trianon.

1935   Hungarian-born Adolph Zukor became the chairman of the Paramount Pictures Corporation. He became one of the greatest film producers in Hollywood.

1938   August 16-19. Two hundred and eighty-three Hungarian-American delegates representing 283 Hungarian-American organizations attended the Second International Congress of Hungarians in Budapest.

1939   The delegation of Americans of Hungarian origin presented
to the New York Historical Society a plaque of Lieutenant
Kovats, the Hungarian-born hero of the War of Independence.
The plaque had been executed by Alexander Finta, a Hungarian-born artist.

The American Hungarian People's Voice (Amerikai Magyar
Nepszava) celebrated its fortieth anniversary. A special
jubilee edition contained congratulatory messages from
President Roosevelt, Governor Lehman, and a number of
prominent Hungarian societies.

Edmund Vasváry, a dedicated researcher of Hungarian materials in the United States, compiled a work entitled Lincoln's Hungarian Heroes: The Participation of Hungarians
in the Civil War. He has collected approximately 375 volumes of materials and compiled a card catalogue of biographical and bibliographical data arranged in about 12,000
entries. In 1974, he received the Abraham Lincoln Award
of the American Hungarian Studies Foundation.

1940   Ferenc Molnár, the well-known Hungarian playwright and
novelist, arrived in America. His best-known play, Liliom,
inspired both the musical and the film Carousel. Many of
his witty and elegant comedies were successfully performed
in America and England in English translation.

1941   January 7. The American Hungarian Federation sent a declaration to the president before the United States entered
the Second World War. The purpose of the announcement
was to start a movement for the preservation of an independent and free Hungary.

The American Hungarian Federation started submitting
memoranda to the president and the secretary of state. By
1949, ten of them had been submitted. In these memoranda
the American Hungarian Federation sought to safeguard the
interests of the people of the Old Country and those living
in the United States who had not yet declared their intent to
become citizens of the United States and received their first
papers.

1943   During the Second World War, there were thousands of Hungarians who served in the United States Armed Forces.
Mrs. John Hegedus received from the mayor of Cleveland
a banner honoring her seven sons who served in the military.

1944   The First Hungarian Evangelistic Reformed Church of Detroit published a memorial volume on its fortieth anniversary. It contained the names of 1,053 adult members, of which 127 were in military service during the Second World War. These soldiers represented approximately 12 percent of the adult congregation. If this percentage is representative of the total population of Hungarian-Americans in 1944, then about 50,000 Hungarians were in military service during the Second World War.

1945   The American Hungarian Federation started the Hungarian Relief Program. A total of $1,457,743 was sent to the needy people of Hungary in the form of money, clothing, and drugs.

At the end of the Second World War, the American government assumed custody of the Crown of St. Stephen and the concomitant crown jewels and treasures. These objects symbolized the thousand-year existence of Hungary as a Christian kingdom. They had been turned over to American authorities in Germany by the Hungarian crown guards who had left Hungary in the closing days of the war.

Béla Bartók, the world-famous composer and musician, died in virtual poverty in New York City. He had in the late 1930s left a secure and respectable existence in Hungary and gone into voluntary exile because of his political and moral convictions. (By his departure, he meant to protest the gradual drifting of Hungary into a rightist orbit and the consequent restrictions on art as well as impending political and racial discrimination.) Bartók had been for nearly a half century one of the most original, productive, and gripping composers of modern classical music rooted in Hungarian folk music, which his researches with Kodály had helped to identify and to distinguish from gypsy and non-Hungarian ethnic admixtures. His famed monograph on the folk music of Hungary and adjacent countries established categories and methods of analysis which still serve as models for contemporary researchers and musicologists. He was a man who successfully synthesized scholarship and creativity, art and morality, thought and feeling. Eighteen years later, the Béla Bartók Archives were established in New York City to promote an understanding and appreciation of his life and work.

After the Second World War

1947   Cardinal Mindszenty, the Roman Catholic Primate of Hun-
            gary, visited the United States and toured some of the Hun-
            garian communities for the first time.

1948   As a result of the Second World War, thousands of Hungar-
            ians lived in camps throughout West Germany. These peo-
            ple were classified as Displaced Persons, and 13,123 of
            them entered the United States under the Displaced Persons
            Act of 1948. They were mostly professionals; and, though
            most of them had to master English, their adjustment to
            American life was comparatively rapid and their contribu-
            tions to their new country were numerous. They also be-
            came a leaven in the activities of Hungarian-American so-
            cieties.

1950   The Golden Jubilee Album of the American Hungarian Peo-
            ple's Voice listed forty-five Hungarian-language newspapers,
            as well as two English-language publications by Hungarians,
            in the United States.

1951   The first Hungarian Boy Scout group in the United States
            was organized by Ferenc Beodray and Ede Csaszar. In the
            same year, the headquarters for the Hungarian Boy Scouts
            moved from Europe to the United States. Fifteen years la-
            ter, in 1966, 1,000 boy and girl scouts camped in Raccoon
            Creek State Park, Pennsylvania.

1953   The Clevelandi Magyar Szabadegyetem (Hungarian Univer-
            sity Extension of Cleveland) was organized by Ferenc So-
            mogyi. Since then, this extension program has offered ten
            college-level lectures annually.

1954   The American Hungarian Studies Foundation was established
            in Elmhurst, Illinois, and later moved to New Brunswick, New
            Jersey, to promote understanding and appreciation of the Hun-
            garian cultural and historical heritage in the United States as
            well as to support and promote publications, research and edu-
            cational programs, and academic studies of Hungarian culture,
            history, music, art, literature, and language in American uni-
            versities, colleges, and high schools. The foundation's museum
            and library contain more than 25,000 volumes and close to
            1,000 museum objects.

1955   According to the almanac of the Catholic Hungarians' Sunday there were 238 Hungarian Catholic priests and 170 Hungarian Catholic churches in America.

After the Hungarian Revolution of 1956

1956   The Hungarian Revolution broke out in Budapest on October 23. During the short but costly fight against the Hungarian Communist regime and the Soviet Russian army, approximately 25,000 died. Subsequently, 40,000 were deported or imprisoned while 200,000 left Hungary. The aim of the majority of revolutionaries, including the short-lived government of Imre Nagy, was to establish a truly democratic socialist republic free of Soviet Russian occupation and domination. The revolutionaries wanted Hungary to be politically and economically as neutral and unaligned as it was practically feasible in the Cold War. As every student of modern Central European history knows, the Soviet Russian occupation troops temporarily left Budapest but reinvaded it on November 4, and restored a pro-Russian Communist regime, which has in recent years turned out to be comparatively liberal and progressive but still retains a quasidictatorial character.

The reaction of the American people to the Soviet Russian invasion of Hungary was instantaneous and massive. In most of the large cities in the United States, the people protested against the subjugation of Hungary. More than 10,000 people gathered in Madison Square Garden and collected close to $1,000,000 for relief for Hungarians.

The Hungarian Revolution made headlines in the American press during this year and years to come. Life, the well-known and now defunct picture magazine, published a special issue about the revolution entitled "Hungary's Fight for Freedom." All the profits from this issue were given to the International Rescue Committee, Inc.

The lasting impact of the Hungarian Revolution on American society is reflected by the number of publications devoted to it in the United States. I. L. Halász de Béky's bibliographies list 1,657 English-language entries up to 1965.

Cardinal Mindszenty, who had been convicted of treason and imprisoned by the Hungarian government in 1948, was temporarily freed during the Hungarian Revolution. When the Revolution failed, he took refuge with the American Legation in Hungary.

1957   The American Hungarian Federation activated the second Hungarian Relief Program for the refugees of the recent

Hungarian Revolution, providing $512,560. With the support of the American Hungarian Federation, 35,705 refugees arrived in the United States.

Many of the Hungarian refugees of 1956 ended up in the United States. Some of them started new organizations while others blended into already existing groups. One of the largest organizations, the Hungarian Freedom Fighters' Association, was established this year. Since then, this organization has held several national conventions on a regular basis.

Among the Hungarian refugees, there were 3,000 college students who later studied at American universities. These students founded the Association of Hungarian Students in North America. This organization published a periodical entitled The Hungarian Student.

1958   The United States Postal Service issued, in the Champion of Liberty series, Louis Kossuth stamps at four and eight cents.

Hungarian musicians -- composers, instrumentalists, and vocalists -- have traditionally been in abundance at home and abroad, in serious, semi-classical, and popular music. To illustrate their impact on American society, we may point out that four of the major symphony orchestras in America during the late 1950s had Hungarian music directors: Eugene Ormandy (Philadelphia Orchestra), George Szell (Cleveland Symphony Orchestra), Fritz Reiner (Chicago Symphony Orchestra), and Antal Dorati (Minneapolis Symphony Orchestra). Dorati has since left the United States, but returned to become Music Director of the National Symphony Orchestra in Washington, D.C.

1959   June 17. The Hungarian Alumni Association was founded at Ohio University, Athens, Ohio. Its aims were to bring Hungarian professionals into closer association, to encourage and promote co-operation among them, and to provide assistance to students of Hungarian origin.

1960   István Serényi, the famous liberty distance runner, made his first commemorative run in eight days from New York to Washington, D.C. In 1962, he accomplished his 74-day, 3,200 mile walk from San Francisco to New York, wearing Hungarian colors. His commemorative runs add up to more than 100,000 miles. He received the Gold Key to New York City and Mt. Vernon as well as the Freedom Awards in both the United States and England.

1961   The first Annual Hungarian Congress of Professionals was organized by the Hungarian Association of Cleveland headed by János Nádas. Also, the Árpád Academy Award was established to encourage Hungarian-related artistic and scientific projects. Since then, the proceedings of the congress have been published every year.

1962   The first History of American Hungarian Literature was compiled by Leslie Könnyü and published in New York.

Edward Teller, a Hungarian-born and Hungarian-trained physicist, received the Fermi Award. To illustrate the contributions of native Hungarians to the physical sciences, three of the nine recipients of the Atom for Peace Award were Hungarians: G.C. Hevesy, L. Szilard, and E.P. Wigner; also, three of nine recipients of the Fermi Award were Hungarians: J. Neumann, E.P. Wigner, and E. Teller.

1963   The first formal Hungarian Who's Who was published in New York under the title Hungarians in America: a Bibliographical Directory of Professionals of Hungarian Origin in the Americas. Edited by Tibor Szy, it listed approximately 6,500 professionals. Since that time two new editions have been published.

1964   The Danubian Press, located in Florida, established the American Hungarian Literary Guild to promote and publish Hungarian literature and history in English. In the United States, there are more than a dozen Hungarian printing presses in operation. They print approximately 400 books, pamphlets, bulletins, and other publications each year.

1966   Miss Maria Judith Reményi of Hungarian origin became Miss U.S.A., and represented the United States in the Miss Universe Contest in Miami, Florida.

1967   Hungarian American librarians held their first meeting at Maryland University. There are approximately 500 librarians of Hungarian origin in America.

The six hundred years of Hungarian university education were celebrated with an exhibition at the University of Maryland.

This year witnessed the death of Zoltán Kodály, the great
Hungarian composer, at the age of 85. Together with Bela
Bartók, Kodály had helped to collect Hungarian and other
Central European folksongs and to write the history of Hungarian folk music. At the same time, like Bartók, he had
become a celebrated composer writing classical music
based on the folk music of Hungary. This is especially evident in his numerous vocal compositions. Unlike Bartok,
Kodály chose to remain in Hungary during and after the
Second World War. He helped to revise the curriculum and
methodology of music education throughout Hungary with
special reference to sightsinging and choral singing in the
lower grades. This curriculum and methodology has been
adopted in various places in the United States. (There is a
Kodály Musical Training Institute at Wellesley, Massachusetts.) Kodály visited America several times -- for the last
time shortly before his death. On this tour he attended numerous gala receptions hosted by musical and public personages and institutions, and he also had the opportunity
of hearing his compositions performed at gala concerts by
the most famous musical organizations under the most
prominent conductors. He is said to have remarked once,
with lasting effect in America, that Hungarians living abroad
are the eighth Hungarian tribe (the other seven tribes being
the original settlers of Hungary in the ninth century).

1968   According to this year's data, there were altogether
            14,500,000 native Hungarians. Nine million, nine hundred
            thousand reside in Hungary while the remainder live in other
            countries, nearly one million of them in the western hemisphere.

1969   The Hungarian Freedom Fighters' Federation, Inc., collected money from Hungarian Americans to erect a monument
            in Los Angeles to commemorate the Freedom Fighters of
            1956. The monument was designed by Árpád Domján and is
            the third largest in the United States.

            The Hungarian communities and press celebrated the
            1000th anniversary of the birth of Saint Stephen (969-1038).
            the first king of Hungary.

1970   The first Hungarian Native Language Congress was held in
            Debrecen, Hungary. The aim of the conference was to upgrade Hungarian language education abroad and to encourage
            cultural exchange between Hungary and Hungarian commun-

ities outside of Hungary, but the congress did not include representatives,i.e. of Hungarians living in the neighboring countries,i.e., Czechoslovakia, the Soviet Union, Romania, and Yugoslavia,where there are 3,300,000 native Hungarians. The Hungarian-American press is constantly concerned about the lack of involvement of Hungarians in these countries and about the one-sided cultural exchange offered by the congress. Approximately thirty Hungarian-American delegates attended this congress.

1971 The American Hungarian Cultural Center of Washington, together with the departments of Languages and Linguistics, Music, and History of the American University, sponsored a lecture series in Washington, D.C. Participants were Antal Doráti, conductor; C.A. Macartney, Professor at the University of Edinburgh, England; Eleanor Lansing Dulles, Professor at Georgetown University, Duke University Research Fellow at the Hoover Institution; and Frenc Nagy, former Prime Minister of Hungary.

It became publicly known that the United States Department of State was using the Crown of St. Stephen and the concomitant crown jewels in American custody as a bargaining factor in negotiating with the Hungarian government. Hungarian-American associations and individuals protested against this tactic to the United States government. Since then, the Hungarian-American press has continually treated this subject.

Denis Gábor, a Hungarian-born physicist, received the Nobel Prize for physics. Other Hungarian-American Nobel Prize winners are George V. Bekessy, for medicine and physiology, 1961; Albert Szent-Györgyi, for medicine and physiology, 1937; and Eugene Wigner, for physics, 1963.

After voluntarily imprisoning himself for fifteen years at the American Legation in Hungary, Cardinal Mindszenty left Hungary because of pressure from the United States government and the Vatican, both of which were trying to reach an accommodation with the present government of Hungary.

1972 Hungarian librarians in the United States and Canada established a forum at the Annual Hungarian Congress in Cleveland to discuss Hungarian-related library topics, and to survey Hungarian collections in America.

The Hungarian communities and the Hungarian press celebrated the 750th anniversary of the Golden Bull, frequently
called the Magna Carta of Hungary.

At the Annual Hungarian Congress, the Hungarian university
professors (approximately 800) in the United States established an informal organization to survey and to encourage
Hungarian studies at American universities.

1973   Cardinal Mindszenty visited the United States for the second
            time and went to New Brunswick for four days.

A park was named after Charles Zágonyi, in Springfield,
Missouri, to commemorate his heroic conduct during the
cavalry charge near Springfield by Union soldiers.

There was a book exhibition, commemorating the 500 years
of Hungarian printing, at the Chicago Public Library, supported by Louis Szathmáry.

The Harvard Circle for Hungarian Studies was formed by
students and faculty interested in Hungarian culture. The
circle has since then sponsored several lectures and meetings with guest speakers such as Béla Bartók, Jr., Pulitzer
Prize winner W.D. Snodgrass, pianist Tibor Szász, and
physician Tibor Ham (president of the American-Hungarian
Cultural Center).

Bishop Zoltán Béky was feted for his forty-five years of devoted service to the American Hungarian Reformed Church
by Hungarian communities all over the United States. The
city of Trenton, New Jersey, named a street after him
(Béky Drive).

March 29. On the 125th anniversary of the Hungarian War
of Independence and the 150th anniversary of the birth of
Sandor Petöfi, Hungary's greatest lyric poet, Bishop Zoltan
Béky opened a session of the House of Representatives with
a prayer.

1974   In the spirit of the coming bicentennial, the Hungarian-
            Americans and Congress commemorate the 250th anniver-
            sary of the birth of the Hungarian-American hero of the
            Revolutuionary War, Colonel Michael de Kovats.

May 6-June 29. The eighty-two-year-old Cardinal Mind-

szenty visited the United States for the third time while on
a world mission of touring Hungarian communities. During
his tour he visited almost all the Hungarian-American communities and met with several high American officials. In
view of the reaction of the news media, Mindszenty had a
great impact on the American society. His memoirs were
published in English translation by Macmillan this year and
became a bestseller.

October 23. John J. Gilligan, Governor of Ohio, designated
this day as Hungarian Freedom Fighters' Day in Ohio, in
memory of the Hungarian Revolution of 1956.

The American Hungarian Federation published a two-volume
set containing the speeches and correspondences of various
distinguished members of the United States Senate and House
of Representatives with reference to the Hungarian question.

December 13. A bill was passed in the Senate, in response
to energetic lobbying by the American Hungarian Federation,
on the basis of a text drafted by Szabolcs Mesterházy. The
bill provides that any country desirous of acquiring the status of "most favored nation" in the United States must agree
to allow the free emigration of its citizens who wish to join
their relatives in the United States. This bill was submitted by Jesse Helms (R-North Carolina) and is humorously
referred to as "the Hungarian Amendment."

Currently, there are sixty-two Hungarian-language newspapers, periodicals, bulletins, and newsletters supported
by the Hungarian communities in the United States. Seventeen of these were established more than half a century
ago: e.g., Szabadság (Liberty), Cleveland (83 years old);
Katolikus Magyarok Vasárnapja (Catholic Hungarians' Sunday), Youngstown (80 years old); and Amerikai Magyar
Népszava (American Hungarian People's Voice), Cleveland
(73 years old).

The United Hungarian Fund reported that in 1973 their capi-
tal was $24,988. The United Hungarian Fund was organized
in 1970 by Loránt Pallos to help needy Hungarians and support Hungarian publications in the United States.

DOCUMENTS

The following documents range from 1583 to 1973, from the historic-
ally attested arrival of the first Hungarian in America to the official cita-
tions of some Hungarian recipients of the Congressional Medal of Honor.
Many, if not all, of the documents are what historians would consider primary sources. They illustrate the research materials upon which my
chronological entries are based. Moreover, they provide a historical fla-
vor and a richness of detail which my paraphrases, condensations, and in-
terpretations necessarily lack. The selection of these documents was dictated partly by their inherent interest and partly by the limitation of space.
The comparatively large number of selections related to the Hungarian
War of Independence is deserving of a few words of explanation. In my view,
which is based on the research and opinions of reputable historians, the
impact of this war and of its aftermath on the United States is a watershed
in the history of American Hungarians. It was upon the arrival in the
United States of Hungarian immigrants in the wake of this war that Hungarian-Americans started to play an increasingly pervasive and important
role in the social, economic, military, and cultural history of this country.

LETTER OF STEPHEN PARMENIUS
1583

Stephen Parmenius of Buda, from Newfound-
land, wrote the following letter to Richard
Hakluyt.

Source: First Published: Richard Hakluyt, The
Principal Navigations Voyages and Discoveries
of the English Nation, London, 1589.

To the worshipfull, Master Richard Hakluit at Oxford in Christchurch
Master of Arts, and Philosophie, his friend and brother.

I had not purposed to write unto you, when the promise of your letters
came to my mind: You thought in June last to have followed us your selfe,
and therefore I had left order that you should be advertised of my state,
by Master Doctor Humfrey: but so you would not be satisfied: I will write
therefore to you almost in the same words, because I have no leasure at
this time, to meditate new matters, and to vary or multiply words.

The 11. of June we set saile at length from England in good earnest,
and departed, leaving the haven and land behind us at Plimmouth: our
Fleete consisted of five shippes: the greatest, which the Admirals brother
had lent us, withdrew her selfe from us the third day, wee know not upon
what occasion: with the rest we sailed still together till the 23. of July: at
which time our view of one another being intercepted by the great mists,
some of us sailed one way, and some another: to us alone the first land
appeared, the first of August, about the latitude of 50. degrees, when as
before we had descended beyond 41. degrees in hope of some Southerly
windes, which notwithstanding never blew to us at any fit time.

It is an Island which your men call Penguin, because of the multitude
of birdes of the same name. Yet wee neither sawe any birds, nor drew
neere to the land, the winds serving for our course directed to another
place, but wee mette altogether at that place a little before the Haven,
whereunto by common Councell we had determined to come, and that
within the space of two houres by the great goodnesse of God, and to our
great joy. The place is situate in Newfound land, betweene 47. and 48.
degrees, called by the name of Saint Johns: the Admirall himselfe by
reason of the multitude of the men, and the smalnesse of his ship, had
his company somewhat sickly, and had already lost two of the same company, which died of the Flixe: of the rest we conceive good hope. Of our
company (for I joyned my selfe with Maurice Browne, a very proper
Gentleman) two persons by a mischance were drowned, the rest are in
safetie, and strong, and for mine owne part I was never more healthy.
Wee arrived at this place the third of August: and the fift the Admirall

tooke possession of the Countrey, for himselfe and the kingdome of England: having made and published certaine Lawes, concerning religion, and obedience to the Queene of England: at this time our fare is somewhat better, and daintier, then it was before: for in good sooth, the experience so long time hath taught us what contrary winds wee have found, and what great travell wee may endure hereafter: and therefore wee will take such order, that wee will want nothing: for we found in this place about twenty Portugall and Spanish shippes, besides the shippes of the English: which being not able to match us, suffer us not to bee hunger starved: the English although they were of themselves strong ynough, and safe from our force, yet seeing our authoritie, by the Queenes letters patents, they shewed us all maner of duety and humanitie.

The maner of this Countrey and people remaine now to be spoken of. But what shall I say, my good Hakluyt, when I see nothing but a very wildernesse? Of fish here is incredible abundance, whereby great gaine growes to them, that travell to these parts: the hooke is no sooner throwne out but it is eftsoones drawne up with some goodly fish: the whole land is full of hilles and woods. The trees for the most part are Pynes and of them some are very olde, and some yong: a great part of them being fallen by reason of their age, doth so hinder the sight of the land, and stoppe the way of those that seeke to travell, that they can goe no whither: all the grasse here is long, and tall, and little differeth from ours. It seemeth also that the nature of this soyle is fit for corne: for I found certaine blades and ears in a manner bearded, so that it appeareth that by manuring and sowing, they may easily be framed for the use of man: here are in the woodes bush berries, or rather straw berries growing up like trees, of great sweetnesse. Beares also appeare about the fishers stages of the Countrey, and are sometimes killed, but they seeme to bee white, as I conjectured by their skinnes, and somewhat lesse than ours. Whether there bee any people in the Countrey I knowe not, neither have I seene any to witnesse it. And to say trueth, who can, when as it is not possible to passe any whither? In like sort it is unknowne, whither any mettals lye under the hilles: the cause is all one, although the very colour and hue of the hilles seeme to have some Mynes in them: we mooved the Admirall to set the woods a fire, that so wee might have space, and entrance to take view of the Countrey, which motion did nothing displease him, were it not for feare of great inconvenience that might thereof insue: for it was reported and confirmed by very credible persons, that when the like happened by chance in another Port, the fish never came to the place about it, for the space of 7. whole yeeres after, by reason of the waters made bitter by the Turpentine, and Rosen of the trees, which ranne into the rivers upon the firing of them. The weather is so hote this time of the yeere, that except the very fish, which is layd out to be dryed by the sunne, be every day turned, it cannot possibly bee preserved from burning: but how cold it is in the winter, the great heapes, and mountaines of yce, in the middest of the Sea have taught us: some of our company report, that in May, they were sometimes kept in, with such huge yce, for 16. whole dayes together, as that the Islands thereof were threescore fathoms thicke, the sides wherof which were toward the Sunne, when they were melted, the whole masse or heape was so inverted and turned in maner of balancing, that that part which was before downeward rose upward, to the great perill of those that are neere them, as by reason wee may gather. The ayre upon land is indifferent cleare, but at Sea toward the East there is nothing els but perpetuall mists, and in the Sea it selfe, about the Banke (for so they call the place where they find ground fourty leagues distant from the shore, and where they beginne to fish) there is no day without raine. When we have served, and supplied our necessitie in this place, we purpose by the helpe of God to passe towards the South, with so much the more hope every day, by how much the greater the things are, that are reported of those Countreys, which we go to discover. Thus much touching our estate.

Now I desire to know somewhat concerning you, but I feare in vaine, but specially I desire out of measure to know how my Patrone master Henry Umpton doth take my absence: my obedience, and duetie shall alwayes bee ready toward him as long as I live: but in deede I hope, that this journey of ours shalbe profitable to his intentions. It remaineth that you thinke me to be still yours, and so yours as no mans more. The sonne of God blesse all our labors, so farre, as that you your selfe may be partaker of our blessing. Adieu, my most friendly, most sweete, most vertuous Hakluyt: In Newfound land, at Saint Johns Port, the 6. of August. 1583.

Steven Parmenius of
Buda, yours.

MICHAEL KOVATS DE FABRICY'S LETTER
TO BENJAMIN FRANKLIN

Michael Kovats de Fabricy wrote asking for
a passport and a letter of recommendation
to Congress.

Source: Coloman Revesz, Colonel-Commandant Michael de Kovats, Drillmaster of Washington's Cavalry, Pittsburgh: Verhovay Fraternal Insurance Association, 1954. (The original Latin letter is on file in the library of
the American Philosophical Society of Philadelphia.)

MOST ILLUSTRIOUS SIR:

"GOLDEN FREEDOM CANNOT BE PURCHASED WITH YELLOW
GOLD"

I, who have the honor to present this letter to your Excellency, am
also following the call of the Fathers of the Land, as the pioneers of
Freedom always did. I am a free man and a Hungarian. As to my military status I was trained in the Royal Prussian Army and raised from the
lowest rank to the dignity of a Captain of the Hussars, not so much by
luck and the mercy of chance than by most diligent self-discipline and
the virtue of my arms. The dangers and the bloodshed of a great many
campaigns taught me how to mould a soldier and, when made, how to arm
him and let him defend the dearest of the lands with his best ability under
any conditions and developments of the war.

I now am here of my own free will, having taken all the horrible hard-
ships and bothers of this journey, and I am willing to sacrifice myself
wholly and most faithfully as it is expected of an honest soldier facing the
hazards and great dangers of the war, to the detriment of Joseph and as
well for the freedom of your great congress. Through the cooperation and
loyal assistance of Mr. Faedevill, a merchant of this city and a kind
sympathizer of the Colonies and their just cause, I have obtained passage
on a ship called, "Catharina Froam Darmouth", whose master is a Captain Whippy. I beg your Excellency to grant me a passport and a letter of
recommendation to the most benevolent Congress. I am expecting companions who have not yet reached here. Your Excellency would be pro-
moting the common cause by giving Mr. Faedevill authorization to expedite their passage to the Colonies once they have arrived here.

At last, awaiting your gracious answer, I have no wish greater than to leave forthwith, to be where I am needed most, to serve and die in everlasting obedience to Your Excellency, and the Congress.

FAITHFUL UNTO DEATH

MICHAEL KOVATS DE FABRICY

Bordeaux, January 13th, 1777

P.S. As yet I am unable to write fluently in French or English and had only the choice of writing either in German or Latin; for this I apologize to your Excellency.

DOCUMENTS RELATED TO THE HUNGARIAN WAR OF INDEPENDENCE OF 1848-49 AND TO KOSSUTH'S TOUR OF THE UNITED STATES

Petition of Hungarian Americans to the president of the United States, to recognize Hungary as an independent state in 1849.

Source: United States, Congress. Senate. Executive Documents, No. 43 (31st Congress, 1st Session)

Mr. L. R. Breisach to the President of the United States.

New York, June 9, 1849.

DEAR SIR: I take the liberty to present this humble petition, which is dictated by pure patriotism in me, a Hungarian by birth, who have lived for two years in this happy country of America, and who admires the principles by which this great republic is ruled.

We, a very small number of Hungarians, residing in New York, united some weeks ago in celebrating the glorious victories of our countrymen in the Old World; and we agreed to send home a flag as a token of our sympathy. On this occasion, the declaration of independence of the Hungarians was noticed by me; and, as all the European papers authenticated this fact, I offered at a subsequent meeting the following propositions to my countrymen, viz:

Whereas it is now notorious to the whole world that the Hungarian nation has declared itself free and independent, the Hungarians of this meeting ought to petition the President of the United States, to the effect that the American government do take into consideration the propriety of sending a diplomatic representative to the Hungarian government, which would, no doubt, be happy to enter into commercial treaties with the United States that would open to American vessels the commodious seaport of Fiume.

But as the appointment of such a minister would have to be confirmed by Congress, I altered, at another meeting, my proposition, so as to suggest the appointment of a diplomatic agent.

The small number of my countrymen here, less experienced, perhaps, than myself, not being sufficiently impressed with the urgency of such a petition, I have thought it my duty to present the petition myself. I flatter myself with success, because the policy of the United States in its foreign relations (as is proved by incontestable facts) has hitherto been to recognise every government which has anywhere been able to establish itself. The United States were the first to recognise Don Miguel; they were the first to recognise Texas after the battle of San Jacinto; and they were the first, too, to recognise the French republic.

Hungary (in population and extent equal to Prussia) stood in the same relation to Austria that the United States stood to England; and she will be happy to make commercial treaties more favorable to the United States than to England, which latter country stands at this time indifferent to the violation of the law of nations by the Russian Emperor.

As at this moment the moral impression on my countrymen, of seeing a native American going to Hungary to offer her the recognition of the United States, would be deep and lasting, I solicit your Excellency to take into consideration my humble petition, which, on my part, has not been influenced by any personal interest.

I remain, with the highest respect, your Excellency's most humble and obedient servant,

L. R. BREISACH,
40 Hudson street; New York

To his Excellency ZACHARY TAYLOR,
    President of the United States of America.

The reply of John M. Clayton (Secretary of State) to L. R. Breisach, regarding the petition of the Hungarian Americans.

Source: United States. Congress. Senate. Executive Documents, No. 43. (31st Congress, 1st Session)

Secretary of State to Mr. Breisach.

DEPARTMENT OF STATE,
Washington, June 25, 1849.

SIR: I am requested by the President to acknowledge the receipt of your letter to him of the 9th instant, and the printed account of the proceedings of the meeting of the Hungarians and others in New York. These proceedings have not escaped attention.

The government and people of this country are profoundly interested in the events which are now passing in Hungary, and all information calculated to throw light on the present struggle between that country and Austria and Russia, cannot fail to be welcome. It is the policy and practice of the United States to recognise all governments which exhibit to the world convincing proofs of their power to maintain themselves. If Hungary sustains herself in this unequal contest, there is no reason why we should not recognise her independence. Congress, it is believed, would sanction such a measure, and this government would be most happy in that event to enter into commercial as well as diplomatic relations with independent Hungary.

I am, sir, very respectfully, your obedient servant,

JOHN M. CLAYTON

L. R. Breisach, Esq.,
  No. 40 Hudson Street, New York.

LETTERS OF A. DUDLEY MANN (special agent to Hungary)
to JOHN M. CLAYTON, Secretary of State

Source: Affairs of Hungary, 1849-1850. United
States. Congress. Senate. Documents 279 (61st
Congress 2nd Session)

Mr. Mann to the Secretary of State.

No. 4.]   Vienna, August 17, 1849

Hon. JOHN M. CLAYTON,
    Secretary of State, Washington.

SIR: A telegraphic despatch just received from Haynau announces that
Gorgey, with his army of 30,000 or 40,000 men, laid down his arms on the
13th instant at Vilagos, an interior town near Arad. No details are given
nor will any probably be received here in an authentic form before to-morrow. It is understood, however, that the surrender was made to a Russian
general.

Within the last week the Magyars experienced several reverses in en-
gagements with Haynau, which, perhaps, counterbalanced the recent advantages obtained by them at Komorn. Should the intelligence respecting Gorgey be confirmed, hostilities can scarcely fail to terminate at an early day
adversely to Hungarian independence.

A rumor originating either in the London Post or Augsburg Gazette is
currently circulated here that the President of the United States had form-
ally received a minister from the government of Kossuth. Fortunately
your note to Mr. L.B. Breisach, under date of June 25, as contained in the
American newspapers, was received yesterday and will place the matter
before the public in its true light. The uniform policy of our Government
with respect to the recognition of foreign states, so succinctly explained in
this note, can not fail to impress all concerned in the question of Hungary
as eminently just and proper.

I transmit this by mail to our despatch agent in London, and I trust it
will arrive in time for the Liverpool steamer of the 25th.

I have the honor to be, most faithfully,
            Your obedient servant,   A. DUDLEY MANN.

Mr. Mann to the Secretary of State.

No. 5.   Vienna, August 24, 1849

HON. JOHN M. CLAYTON,
          Secretary of State, Washington.
     SIR: The surrender of Gorgey, according to the report of Paskiewitsch
to the Czar, was unconditional. Not a paragraph relative to this momen-
tous occurrence has yet been published by order of the Austrian Government.
Detailed official accounts, however, were received here this morning from
Warsaw, where they appeared in the "Courier" of the 18th instant. The
following is a translation of the report of Taskiewitsch:

> Hungary lies at the feet of your imperial majesty!
>
> The government of the insurgents in its act of dis-
> solution transferred all power to Gorgey, who, uncon-
> ditionally, surrendered to the Russian army. The
> other insurgent commanders will undoubtedly follow
> his example. The officers sent by Gorgey to me to
> negotiate a capitulation appeared to be willing to
> proceed to them with commissioners from our army,
> or from that of Austria, to endeavor to occasion a
> discontinuance of hostilities.
>
> I am most fortunate in being enabled to report to
> your imperial majesty that the only request made of
> me by Gorgey was for the enjoyment of the privilege
> of surrendering to your army.
>
> I have made suitable arrangements for having the
> troops of Gorgey surrounded by the corps of General
> Rüdiger, to which the disarming of it is confided.
>
> With regard to the delivery of the prisoners, and
> the arrangements for the other insurgents who may
> lay down their arms, I will advise with the comman-
> der in chief of the Austrian army. I have had Gorgey
> brought to my headquarters, where he shall remain
> until I receive further orders from your imperial
> majesty.

     It seems to be pretty well authenicated that a Hungarian war council
was held at Arad on the 11th of August, in which all the members of the
Government participated. That at the commencement of its deliberations
Gorgey expressed a belief that recent reverses left no alternative to the
Magyars but an abandonment of the cause for which they were struggling.
That Kossuth, giving utterance to opinions diametrically opposite, was over-
ruled by a considerable majority, and bowing to the will of that majority,
immediately, by public proclamation, notified his countrymen that his offi-
cial life was terminated, inasmuch as Gorgey had been chosen dictator.
And that the first use Gorgey made of the authority conferred upon him was

to place Hungary "at the feet of his imperial majesty, " the Emperor of all the Russias.

The remark of the "Presse, " made at the time the news from Vilagos was gazetted, that "We are at a loss which to admire most, the military or diplomatic skill of General Paskiewitsch, " has become quite proverbial. It receives additional point from the fact that Hungary, as reported by the prince, is prostrate before the Czar, and that the only condition required in the consummation of this deed was an exclusive surrender to the Russian army.

Kossuth, it is stated, started the same day that he was divested of his authority to Orsova, in Turkey. Whether in future he is to play a great role in the management of the affairs of eastern Europe the Almighty in His wisdom must determine. Gorgey will assuredly be placed in a high military position, either in the Russian or Austrian service, as it is admitted on all sides that his professional talents are of a very superior order. All will depend, as respects the arms which he is to bear hereafter, upon the partition or disposition, as a whole, of Hungary. Between Kossuth and Gorgey, in political sentiment, there was never any sympathy. The latter was an uncompromising monarchist, as is distincly seen in recent developments. Under the mask of national independence he fought for individual glory, not for liberal government. Consequently he was the idol of Magyar nobility, and in the war council the nobility prevailed. Kossuth, after the capture of Pesth, lost all control over the movements of Gorgey and therefore suspected his loyalty, communicating his suspicions to Benn.

The reports of Haynau and Paskiewitsch -- the former to the Austrian and the latter to the Russian Emperor -- relative to the victories of Vilagos, Arad, etc., have this moment made their appearance. I regret that I have not time before, the last post for the steamer starts, to furnish you with a translation of them. I send herewith the evening edition of the Presse containing them. It will be seen that Haynau claims for the Austrians the glory of hastening the war to a close.

The Augsburg Gazette and other papers contain a translation of your note upon the subject of the recognition of Hungary.

I have the honor to be, most faithfully,

Your obedient servant,   A. DUDLEY MANN.

RESOLUTIONS OF SYMPATHY WITH THE CAUSE OF HUNGARIAN LIBERTY

Source: A Lincoln's Collected Works, II.
Rutger's University Press, 1953-55.

September 6. 1849.

Resolved, That in their present glorious struggle for liberty, the Hungarians command our highest admiration and have our warmest sympathy.

Resolved, That they have our most ardent prayers for their speedy triumph and final success.

Resolved, That the Government of the United States should acknowledge the independence of Hungary as a nation of freemen at the very earliest moment consistent with our amicable relations with the government against which they are contending.

Resolved, That in the opinion of this meeting, the immediate acknowledgment of the independence of Hungary by our government is due from American freemen to their struggling brethren, to the general cause of republican liberty, and not violative of the just rights of any nation or people.

Resolutions in Behalf of Hungarian Freedom
(January 9, 1852.)

Whereas, in the opinion of this meeting, the arrival of Kossuth in our country, in connection with the recent events in Hungary, and with the appeal he is now making in behalf of his country, presents an occasion upon which we, the American people, cannot remain silent, without justifying an inference against our continued devotion to the principles of our free institutions, therefore,

Resolved, 1. That it is the right of any people, sufficiently numerous for national independence, to throw off, to revolutionize, their existing form of government, and to establish such other in its stead as they may choose.

2. That it is the duty of our government to neither foment, nor assist, such revolutions in other governments.

3. That, as we may not legally or warrantably interfere abroad, to aid, so no other government may interfere abroad, to suppress such revolutions; and that we should at once, announce to the world, our determinations to insist upon this mutuality of non-intervention, as a sacred principle of the international law.

4. That the late interference of Russia in the Hungarian struggle was, in our opinion, such illegal and unwarrantable interference.

5. That to have resisted Russia in that case, or to resist any power in a like case, would be no violation of our own cherished principles of non-intervention, but, on the contrary, would be ever meritorious, in us, or any independent nation.

6. That whether we will, in fact, interfere in such case, is purely a question of policy, to be decided when the exigency arrives.

7. That we recognize in Governor Kossuth of Hungary the most worthy and distinguished representative of the cause of civil and religious liberty on the continent of Europe. A cause for which he and his nation struggled until they were overwhelmed by the armed intervention of a foreign despot, in violation of the more sacred principles of the laws of nature and of nations— principles held dear by the friends of freedom everywhere, and more especially by the people of these United States.

8. That the sympathies of this country, and the benefits of its position, should be exerted in favor of the people of every nation struggling to be free; and whilst, we meet to do honor to Kossuth and Hungary, we should not fail to pour out the tribute of our praise and approbation to the patriotic efforts of the Irish, the Germans and the French, who have unsuccessfully fought to establish in their several governments the supremacy of the people.

A further resolution was adopted instructing the officers' to have the resolutions published and copies sent to Louis Kossuth and to each Illinois member of Congress.

LETTER OF JOHN M. CLAYTON
1850

The letter of John M. Clayton (Secretary of
State) to George P. Marsh, U.S. Consul in
Constantinople, instructing Marsh to intercede officially with the Sultan on behalf of
escaped Hungarian freedom fighters of 1848-
1849 and offering them transportation to an
asylum in the United States.

Source: United States. Congress. Senate.
Executive Documents, No. 43. (31st Congress,
1st Session)

Secretary of State to Mr. Marsh.

[No. 3.]   DEPARTMENT OF STATE,
                                 Washington, January 12, 1850

SIR: You are well aware that the deepest interest is felt among the
people of the United States in the fate of Kossuth and his compatriots of
Hungary, who have hitherto escaped . . . . . by seeking an asylum within
the boundaries of the Ottoman empire. The accounts respecting them have
been so conflicting -- sometimes representing them as having escaped, and
at others as being captive -- that we have not known what to credit, and have
therefore declined to interfere in their behalf, nor do we now desire to interfere by entangling ourselves in any serious controversy with Russia or
Austria. But we cannot suppose that a compliance with the dictates of humanity, now that the contest with Hungary is over, would involve our friendly relations with any other power. Should you be of the opinion that our
goo doffices would avail anything to secure their safety . . . . . .it is desired by your government that you should intercede with the Sultan in their
behalf. The President would be gratified if they could find a retreat under
the American flag; and their state conveyance to this country by any one of
our national ships which may be about to return home, would be hailed with
lively satisfaction by the American people.
     I am, very respectfully, your obedient servant,
                                 JOHN M. CLAYTON.
Hon. George P. Marsh, &c., Constantinople.

Source: United States. Congress. Senate. Miscellaneous, No. 35. (31st Congress, 1st Session).

| 31st Congress | [SENATE] | Miscellaneous, |
| 1st Session | | No. 35. |

RESOLUTIONS
of
THE LEGISLATURE OF NEW YORK,
in favor of

Granting land to the exiles of Hungary and other European countries, and also to certain citizens of the United States.

January 28, 1850.
Ordered to lie on the table, and be printed.

STATE OF NEW YORK,
IN ASSEMBLY, January 18, 1850.

Whereas a resolution has been introduced in the Senate of the United States, instructing the Committee on Public Lands to inquire and report on the propriety of setting apart a portion of the public domain, to be granted, free of all charges, to the exiles of Hungary, already arrived and hereafter to arrive in the United States, as well as to the exiles fleeing from oppression in other European countries: therefore,

Resolved, (if the Senate concur,) That this legislature is in favor of the measure proposed, and that our senators and representatives are requested to do all in their power to carry it into effect: Provided, The persons receiving the lands shall become actual settlers thereon.

And whereas a large portion of the people of our own country are landless and without homes: therefore,

Resolved, (if the Senate concur,) That our senators be instructed, and our representatives be requested, to make the public lands free, in limited quantities, to all actual settlers who are citizens of the United States, who are not the owners of land, or possessed of the means of purchasing it; Congress to retain the power of making special grants.

Resolved, (if the Senate concur,) That the governor of this State be requested to transmit a copy of the foregoing resolutions to each of our senators and representatives from this State in Congress.

By order of the Assembly:

JAMES R. ROSE, Clerk

STATE OF NEW YORK, in Senate, January 22, 1850

Resolved, That the Senate do concur in the passage of the foregoing resolutions.

By order of the Senate:

WILLIAM H. BOGART, Clerk.

RESOLUTION OF THE LEGISLATURE OF INDIANA
April 8, 1850

Source: United States. Congress. Senate. Miscellaneous, No. 88. (31st Congress, 1st Session).

31st Congress,	SENATE	Miscellaneous,
1st Session		No. 88.

RESOLUTION
of
THE LEGISLATURE OF INDIANA,
In relation to Hungary.

April 8, 1850
Ordered to lie upon the table, and be printed.

JOINT RESOLUTION in relation to the brave and patriotic sons of Hungary.

SECTION 1. Resolved unanimously, That the brave and patriotic people of Hungary are entitled to our warmest sympathy in their unsuccessful
struggle for the liberty of their country against the despots of Austria and
Russia; and that the curelty exhibited by the Emperor of Austria, in the execution of her bravest generals and patriotic ministers of religion, for no
other act than fighting and praying for the liberty of their country, demands
the universal condemnation and execration of all nations.

SEC. 2. And be it further resolved, That it is the duty of the government of the United States of America to make a solemn protest against the
inhuman butchery of the patriots of Hungary by the tyrants of Austria, as
an infraction of the laws of nations, and an insult to the feelings of all free
States.

SEC. 3. And be it further resolved, That we, the representatives of the
State of Indiana, in the name of the people of said State, do enter our solemn protest against the inhuman butchery aforesaid, and request that a cer-
tified copy of these joint resolutions be forwarded by the governor of Indiana to each of our senators and representatives in Congress, with instructions that they recommend the government of the United States to use all
the power and influence of the government, through its ministers at the
courts of Austria and Russia, to obtain an amelioration of the condition of
the brave patriots of Hungary, and that a general pardon be extended to all
those brave men who defended their country and her sacred cause.

GEORGE W. CARR,
Speaker of the House of Representatives.
JAMES H. LANE,
President of the Senate.

Approved January 12, 1850

JOSEPH A. WRIGHT.

PRESIDENT'S MESSAGE (Excerpt)

A message was sent by President Fillmore to
both Houses of Congress concerning the intervention of the United States on behalf of the escaped Hungarian freedom fighters 1848-1849 in
Turkey. The message reads as follows:

Source: The Congressional Globe, December
2, 1851.

. . . The Turkish Government has expressed its thanks for the kind
reception given to the Sultan's agent, Amin Bey, on the occasion of his recent visit to the United States. On the 28th of February last, a dispatch
was addressed by the Secretary of State to Mr. Marsh, the American Minister at Constantinople, instructing him to ask of the Turkish government
permission for the Hungarians, then imprisoned within the dominions of
the Sublime Porte, to remove to this country. On the 3d of March last,
both Houses of Congress passed a resolution requesting the President to
authorize the employment of a public vessel to convey to this country
Louis Kossuth and his associates in captivity.

The instruction above referred to was complied with, and the Turkish
Government having released Governor Kossuth and his companions from
prison, on the 10th of September last they embarked on board of the United
States steam-frigate Mississippi, which was selected to carry into effect
the resolution of Congress. Governor Kossuth left the Mississippi at Gi-
braltar, for the purpose of making a vist to England, and may shortly be
expected in New York. By communications to the Department of State he
has expressed his grateful acknowledgments for the interposition of this
Government in behalf of himself and his associates. This country has been
justly regarded as a safe asylum for those whom political events have exiled from their own homes in Europe; and it is recommended to Congress
to consider in what manner Governor Kossuth and his companions, brought
hither by its authority, shall be received and treated. . . .

RECEPTION OF LOUIS KOSSUTH

Reception of Louis Kossuth, former governor
of Hungary, and his suite in the United States
Senate.

Source: The Congressional Globe, January 5,
1852.

RECEPTION OF LOUIS KOSSUTH

At one o'clock the doors of the Senate Chamber were thrown open, and
Governor Kossuth, supported by the committee appointed by the Senate to
introduce him, the Hon. James Shields, the Hon. Wm. H. Seward, and
the Hon. Lewis Cass, entered and advanced within the bar, the Senate ris-
ing to receive them.

The suite of Governor Kossuth, in military uniforms, were grouped
below the bar.

Mr. SHIELDS addressed the President, as follows:

"Mr. President, we have the honor to introduce Louis Kossuth to the
Senate of the United States."

The PRESIDENT pro tempore then addressed him, as follows:

"Louis Kossuth, I welcome you to the Senate of the United States. The
committee will conduct you to the seat which I have caused to be prepared
for you. "

He was then conducted to a chair in front of the President's desk, and
seated with the Committee of the Senate.

Mr. MANGUM rose some time afterwards and said: Mr. President,
with a view of affording Senators an opportunity of paying their respects
to our illustrious guest, I move that the Senate do now adjourn.

The motion was agreed to.

the PRESIDENT then descended to the floor of the Senate, and was introduced to Governor Kossuth by the committee. The other Senators were
also severally introduced: after which gentlemen and ladies present in
great numbers sought the same gratification. Amongst the incidents of the
levee, it may be mentioned that when the martial figure of General Houston
approached Kossuth, there appeared to be a special attraction in the person of the hero of San Jacinto. The introduction having been made, the
following brief but expressive dialogue ensued:

Mr. HOUSTON. Sir, you are welcome to the Senate of the United
States.

Mr. KOSSUTH. I can only wish I had been as successful as you, sir.

Mr. HOUSTON. God grant that you may yet be so.

Subsequently the distinguished stranger was conducted to the Vice

President's room, to which the President pro tem. and Senators retired
with him.

WELCOMING ADDRESS BY RALPH WALDO EMERSON

Welcoming address delivered by Ralph Waldo
Emerson to Louis Kossuth at Concord, Massachusetts, on May 11, 1852.

Source: Ralph Waldo Emerson, Emerson's Complete Works, Boston: Houghton Mifflin and Co.,
1886. Vol. 11.

Sir: The fatigue of your many public visits, in such un-
broken succession as may compare with the toils of a campaign, forbid us to detain you long. The people of this town
share with their countrymen the admiration of valor and per-
severance; they like their compatriots, have been hungry to
see the man whose extraordinary eloquence is seconded by the
splendor and the solidity of his actions But, as it is the priv-
ilege of the people of this town to keep a hallowed mound
which has a place in the history of the country, we knew beforehand that you would not go by us; you could not take all
your steps in the pilgrimage of American liberty, until you had
seen with your own eyes the ruins of the little bridge where a
handful of brave farmers opened our revolution. Therefore,
we sat and waited for you.

And now, sir, we are heartily glad to see you at last in
these fields. We set no more value than you do on cheers and
huzzas. But we think that the graves of our heroes around us
throb today to a footstep that sounded like their own:

"The mighty tread,
Brings from the dust the sound of liberty."

Sir, we have watched with attention your progress
through the land, and the varying feeling with which you have
been received, and the unvarying tone and countenance you
have maintained. We wish to discriminate in our regard. We
wish to reserve our honor for actions of the noblest strain.

We please ourselves that in you we meet with one whose tem-
per was long since tried in fire, and made equal to all events;
a man so truly in love with a glorious fortune, that he can not
be divereted to any less.

It is our republican doctrine, too, that the wide variety
of opinions is an advantage. I believe I may say, of the people
of this country at large, that sympathy is more worth, because
it stands the test of party. It is not a blind wave; it is a living
soul, contending with living souls. It is in every expression
antagonized. No opinion will pass, but must stand the tug of
war. As you see, the love you win is worth something, for it
has been argued through; its foundation searched; it has proved sound and whole; it may be avowed; it will last; and it will
draw all opinion to itself.

We have seen with great pleasure that there is nothing accidental in your attitude. We have seen that you are organically in that cause you plead. The man of freedom, you are also a man of fate. You do not elect, but you are elected by God and your genius to your task. We do not, therefore, affect to thank you. We only see in you the angel of freedom, crossing sea and land; crossing parties, nationalities, private interests, and self-esteems; dividing populations, where you go, and drawing to your part only the good. We are afraid you are growing popular, sir; you may be called to the dangers of prosperity. But hitherto you have had, in all countries and in all parties, only the men of heart. I do not know but you will have the million yet. Then, may your strength be equal to your day! But remember, sir, that everything great and excellent in the world is in minorities.

Far be it fom us, sir, any tone of patronage; we ought rather to ask yours. We know the austere condition of liberty, that it must be re-conquered over and over again; yea, day by day, that it is a state of war; that it is always slipping from those who boast it to those who fight for it; and you, the foremost soldier of freedom, in this age; — it is for us to crave your judgement; who are we, that we should dictate to you? You have won your own. We only affirm it. This country of working-men greet you a worker. This republic greets in you a republican. We only say. "Well done, good and faithful". You have earned your own nobility at home. We admit you ad eundem, as they say at college; we admit you to the same degree, without new trial; we suspend all rules before so paramount a merit. You may well sit a doctor in the college of liberty; you have achieved your right to interpret our Washington. And I speak

the sense, not only of every generous American, but the law of mind, when I say that it is not those who live idly in the city called after his name but those who, all over the world, think and act like him, who may claim to explain the sentiment of Washington.

Sir, whatever obstruction, from selfishness, indifference, or from property — which always sympathizes with possession — you may encounter, we congratulate you that you have learned how to convert calamities into powers, exile into a campaign, present defeat into lasting victory. For this new crusade which you preach to willing and unwilling ears in America is a seed of armed men. You have got your story told in every palace, and log hut, and prairie camp, throughout this continent. And, as the shores of Europe and America approach every month, and their politics will one day mingle, when the crisis arrives, it will find us all instructed beforehand in the rights and wrongs of Hungary, and parties already to her freedom.

THE KOSZTA AFFAIR

This document and the five documents following
are related to the Koszta Affair, which resulted
in a foreign intervention by the United States on
behalf of an immigrant and in the articulation of
a principle of intervention to protect the rights
of American immigrants and residents traveling
abroad. It is worthy of emphasis that this was
the first ultimatum delivered by the United States
to another country on behalf of an immigrant.

Source: United States. Congress, House of
Representatives. Executive Document No. 91.
(33rd Congress, 1st Session).

HO. OF REPS.

| 33d Congress | | EX. DOC. |
| 1st Session | | No. 91. |

MARTIN KOSZTA -- CORRESPONDENCE, &c.

MESSAGE
from
THE PRESIDENT OF THE UNITED STATES,
transmitting
Copies of correspondence, &c., growing out of the seizure and resuce of
Martin Koszta.

April 14, 1854. -- Ordered to be printed.

To the House of Representatives:

I transmit, herewith, a report from the Secretary of State, with accompanying documents, in compliance with the resolution of the House of
Representatives of the 4th instant.

FRANKLIN PIERCE.

Washington, April 12, 1854.

Department of State,
Washington, April 12, 1854.

The Secretary of State, to whom has been referred the resolution of
the House of Representatives of the 4th instant, requesting the President,

"if not inconsistent with the public interest, to transmit to the House of Representatives copies of the correspondence, not now communicated, of the United States legation at Constantinople and the United States consulate at Smyrna with Captain Ingraham, and with the government of Austria, and with this government, together with the instructions from this government to their agents abroad, touching the seizure and rescue of Martin Koszta, and the terms and conditions on which he was liberated and sent to this country, " has the honor to lay before the President a copy of the papers specified in the accompanying list, which, with those sent to the Senate on the 1st of March and the 5th of April, herewith enclosed, embrace all the correspondence on the subject not heretofore communicated to the House of Representatives.

Respectfully submitted:

W.L. MARCY.

To the President of the United States.

A LETTER FROM COMMANDER D. N. INGRAHAM TO J. C. DOBBIN,
SECRETARY OF THE NAVY, GIVING A FULL ACCOUNT OF
THE KOSZTA AFFAIR.

> Source: United States. Congress. House of Rep-
> resentatives. Executive Documents No. 91.
> (33rd Congress, 1st Session).

UNITED STATES SHIP ST. LOUIS,
Smyrna, July 3, 1853

SIR: It becomes my duty to report to you an affair at this place, in
which I have taken upon myself to compromise the American flag.

I arrived here upon the 23d of June, and, soon after anchoring, was
informed that an American had been kidnapped by the Austrian consul upon
the Turkish soil, and sent on board an Austrian brig-of-war.

I sent for the American consul, and informed him of what I had heard.
He told me the man was a Hungarian refugee, (named Martin Koszta,) who
had a certificate of intention to become a citizen of the United States, and
came here in an American vessel, but that he did not consider him under
his protection, having, to his knowledge, no passport.

The consul and myself then went on board the brig and requested to
see the commander, but were told he was not on board. We then went to
the Austrian consul and demanded to see Koszta, which, after some demur,
was granted. After a conversation with Koszta, I was afraid I had no right
to demand him as a citizen of the United States, but determined neither to
make a claim, nor acquiesce in his seizure, until I could hear from the legation at Constantinople. I was guided in this opinion by the consul, who
seemed to think we could not use force without more evidence than the paper
in his possession gave. I then requested the consul to write immediately
to the legation, which he did. Before an answer could arrive, I received
information that Koszta was to be sent to Trieste. I immediately wrote to
the commander of the brig, protesting against this step, and received a
verbal reply that he was ignorant of any such intention. Next morning, at
daylight, I got under way and anchored within half-cable's length of the brig,
and loaded my guns; the steamer, in which it was said Koszta was to be
sent, being very near. At 11 a.m. an answer came from Mr. Brown, stating that Koszta was an American citizen, and advising the consul to give
him all aid and sympathy, but in an unofficial way. I then told the consul
he must insist upon Koszta remaining until I again heard from the charge.
He did so, when the Austrian consul told him he had intended to send the
man that day, but would wait until the next mail. On Saturday, the 2d of
July, the capon ogland of the legation arrived with letters from the charge
to the consul and myself to use stringent measures.

I immediately had an interview with Koszta, in which he claimed the
protection of the American flag. I then addressed note "B" to the comman-

der of the brig, demanding Koszta's release. I also directed the American consul to furnish the Austrian consul with a copy of the demand, which was done.

At this time the Austrian brig and a 10-gun schooner, that arrived the day before, prepared for action; having three mail steamers to assist. I did the same, and awaited the hour of 4 p.m. At 12 our consul came off with a proposition that Koszta should be delivered into the hands of the consul general of France, to be held at the joint order of the American and Austrian consuls until his nationality should be determined. After some consideration, and the advice of the English and French consuls to ours, I agreed to the terms. The prisoner was then landed, amid the cheers of the inhabitants and every demonstration of joy. I know, sir, I have taken a fearful responsibility upon myself by this act; but after Mr. Brown had informed me Koszta had taken the oath of allegiance to the United States, and forsworn all allegiance to Austria; that he was an American citizen, and had been under the protection of the legation at Constantinope, I could not hesitate to believe he was fully entitled to protection. It was a case of life and death, for it Koszta had been taken to Trieste his fate was sealed; and could I have looked the American people in the face again if I had allowed a citizen to be executed, and not used the power in my hands to protect him for fear of doing too much? The easy manner, also, in which he was given up, and the convention that he should be held by a third party until his nationality could be established, is evidence that they were not sure of their ground.

Should my conduct be approved by you, sir, it will be one of the proudest moments of my life, that I have saved this gallant man from a cruel and ignominious death. On the other hand, should the course I have pursued be disavowed, I must bow to the decision; but whatever may be the consequences to myself, I shall feel I have done my best to support the honor of the flag, and not allow a citizen to be oppressed who claimed at my hands the protection of the flag.

I enclose copies of all the papers (A to E) relating to this affair.

I have the honor to be, very respectfully, your obedient servant,

D.N. INGRAHAM,
Commander.

Hon. J.C. Dobbin,
Secretary of the Navy, Washington, D.C.

LETTER FROM J.C. DOBBIN, SECRETARY OF THE NAVY
1853

A letter from J.C. Dobbin, Secretary of the
Navy, approving the course of actions taken
by Commander D.N. Ingraham in the Koszta
affair.

Source: United States. Congress. House of Representatives. Executive Documents No. 91.
(33rd Congress, 1st Session).

U.S. NAVY DEPARTMENT,
Washington, August 19, 1853

SIR: The department acknowledges the receipt of your communication
bearing date the 3d of July, 1853, in which you relate the course you deemed
it your duty to pursue, on being "informed that an American had been kidnapped by the Austrian consul upon the Turkish soil, and sent on board an
Austrian brig-of-war;" and who, upon further investigation, was discovered
to be a Hungarian -- Martin Koszta -- who had, in July, 1852, filed his
declaration to become a citizen of the United States, and had arrived at
Smyrna in an American vessel.

This department does not feel called upon to enlarge upon the various
questions of international law involved in the proceedings adopted by the
officers of the different governments concerned. Thos questions may hereafter become subjects of discussion between the respective governments
interested.

I deem it proper, at present, to content myself by assuring you that
the prudence, promptness, and spirit which marked the part you bore in
the transaction, is approved by this department.

It is a matter of gratulation that the affair terminated without a resort
to collision and bloodshed.

The President desires that, on all occasions and in all parts of the
globe visited by the American navy, the rights and the property of American citizens should be watched over with vigilance and protected with energy; but he, with no less earnestness, enjoins it upon the officers of the
navy to exercise due caution to avoid the slightest infraction of the laws of
nations, and scrupulously regard the rights of others. Respect the flags of
other nations, and with the more pride you can demand respect for your
own.

By the next steamer I may, probably, forward to you a copy of the instructions now in preparation at the State Department for our minister at
Constantinople.

I am, respectfully, your obedient servant,

J.C. DOBBIN.

Commander D.N. Ingraham,
  Commanding U.S. Sloop-of-war St. Louis, Mediterranean.

TWO LETTERS FROM COMMANDER D.N. INGRAHAM TO THE
COMMANDER OF THE HUSSAR

Two letters from Commander D.N. Ingraham to
the Commander of the Hussar, the former stating
that the Hussar should not leave the port until a
decision was received from Constantinople and
the latter demanding the release of Koszta.

Source: United States. Congress. House of Representatives. Executive Documents No. 91.
(33rd Congress, 1st Session).

UNITED STATES SHIP ST. LOUIS,
Smyrna Roads, evening, June 28, 1853.

SIR: I have this moment received a letter stating that Martin Koszta
was to be sent on board the steamer to-morrow, at daylight, to be sent to
Trieste. I have been only waiting to hear from the minister at Constantinople before I took some action in the case of Koszta. As he has a paper
stating his intention of becoming a citizen of the United States, I earnestly
protest against his leaving this port before something has been heard from
Constantinople.

Very respectfully, your obedient servant,
D.M. INGRAHAM
Commander.

To the COMMANDER of the Austrian brig "Hussar."

———

UNITED STATES SHIP ST. LOUIS,
Smyrna, July 2, 1853.

SIR: I have been directed by the American charge at Constantinople
to demand the person of Martin Koszta, a citizen of the United States taken
by force on Turkish soil, and now confined on board the brig "Hussar;"
and if a refusal is given, to take him by force.
An answer to this demand must be returned by 4 o'clock p.m.

Very respectfully, your obedient servant,
D.M. INGRAHAM,
Commander.

To the COMMANDER of the Austrian brig "Hussar."

THE DECLARATION OF KOSZTA

The declaration of Koszta stating his intention
to become a citizen of the United States.

Source: United States. Congress. House of Representatives. Executive Documents No. 91.
(33rd Congress, 1st Session).

1852. -- STATE OF NEW YORK.

In the Court of Common Pleas for the city and county of New York.

I, Martin Koszta, do declare, on oath, that it is bona fide my intention to become a citizen of the United States, and to renounce forever all
allegiance and fidelity to any foreign prince, potentate, State or sovereign-
ty whatever, and particularly to the emperor of Austria, of whom I am a
subject.

MARTIN KOSZTA.

Sworn this 31st day of July, 1852
George W. Riblet, Clerk.

_____

Clerk's office, Court of Common Pleas for the city and county of New York:

I certify that the foregoing is a true copy of an original declaration of
intention, remaining of record in my office.
In witness whereof, I have hereunto signed my name and affixed the
L.S.   seal of said court, this 31st day of July, 1852.

GEORGE W. RIBLET, Clerk.

LETTER FROM E .S. OFFLEY TO WILLIAM L. MARCY
1853

A letter from E .S. Offley to William L. Marcy,
Secretary of State, summarizing the Koszta affair.

Source: United States. Congress. House of Representatives. Executive Documents No. 91.
(33rd Congress, 1st Session).

Mr. Offley to Mr. Marcy.

UNITED STATES CONSULATE, SMYRNA,
July 5, 1853

SIR: I have the honor of laying before you the following occurrence,
which has lately taken place in this city:

Late in the evening of the 22d of June last, I was informed that a Hungarian refugee, with an American passport, had been forcibly arrested by
a band of armed hirelings, who had been employed for this purpose by the
Austrian consul of Smyrna, and they took him on board of the "Hussar, "
an Austrian brig-of-war lying in this port.

I immediately applied to the governor of this city, informing him of
the occurrence, stating that if the refugee who had been arrested was really
the holder of an American passport, I claimed him from the Turkish authorities. Some hours after, at about midnight, a person called on me and
handed me a document which he stated he had taken from the trunk of the
person that had been arrested. This document is a copy of a declaration
made in the court of common pleas for the city and county of New York,
on the 31st day of July, 1852, by Martin Koszta, an Austrian subject, whe
where in he declares, on oath, that it is his intention to become a citizen
of the United States. Martin Koszta is one of the Hungarian refugees who
were kept in "Kutahia, " with Kossuth.

In February last he arrived here from Boston, and shortly after his
arrival called at this consulate to show me the declaration aforementioned,
stating that he intended to remain here for one or two months, and wished
to know if I could, in virtue of said declaration, give him the protection of
this consulate, as a "citizen of the United States, " during his stay here.
I told him that as he had not fulfilled the requirements of the law of naturalization, I could not consider him as an American citizen, but that I would
grant him my unofficial influence in case he might have any difficulties with
the authorities, and advised him to leave this country as soon as possible,
as it would be imprudent for him to stay here without the protection of some
consulate.

On the 23d, the morning after his arrest, the United States corvette

the "St. Louis" came in sight, and on her arrival I went on board and related the circumstances of the case to Commander D.N. Ingraham, who
had already been informed of the arrest by a deputation of refugees, who
had gone on board for that purpose, and who had told him that Koszta was
a citizen of the United States, and that they claimed the protection of the
American flag in his behalf. Under these circumstances, we considered
ourselves bound to go on board the brig and see Koszta, and ask him on
what grounds his friends claimed for him American protection. On our arrival, we asked the officer of the watch if the captain were on board, who
replied that he had gone ashore to see the consul. We then informed the
officer that we had come to see the man who had been seized the day previous, and who was confined on board the brig. He replied that no such
person was there. We then went to the Austrian consul and requested him
to allow us to interrogate Koszta in regard to his nationality, who answered
that as he had given him up to the commander of the brig, he could not interfere in the matter, and that we ought to see the commander of the brig,
where Koszta had been sent after his arrest. We then told him that we had
just come from on board of the brig, and that the officer of the watch had
told us that the commander was at the consulate, and that no such person
had been sent on board of their vessel. This contradictory statement led
us to think that an understanding had taken place between the consul and
commander of the brig, in order that we might not be allowed to see Koszta.
However, we firmly insisted on seeing him, and after many objections the
Austrian consul agreed to send for the commander of the brig, and asked
him if he were willing to allow us to go on board and see Koszta, to which
the commander acceded, and we went on board with him and the consul.
We found Koszta in chains, guarded by two men, and he appeared confused
by the ill treatment of the previous day. We interrogated him on what
grounds his friends claimed for him American protection, and if he had an
American passport; he replied that he had not any, and that he had nothing
but the declaration already mentioned, which he had shown me on his arrival in this city, upon which I left the brig with Commander Ingraham, without our having expressed any opinion on the matter.

On the 24th I addressed a letter to the United States legation at Constantinople, reporting the illegal act committed by the Austrian consul,
in order that it might take such steps as it should deem proper for the

On the evening of the 28th a letter was sent on board the "St. Louis,"
informing Commander Ingraham that Koszta was to be sent next morning,
at daylight, on board the Austrian steamer that was to leave that day for
Trieste, begging his interference in order that this might be hindered. On
receipt of this letter, Commander Ingraham addressed a note to the commander of the brig, acquainting him of the foregoing, and that as he expected to hear from the United States minister at Constantinople in regard
to Koszta's case, he earnestly protested against Koszta being sent away

from this port before then. The commander of the brig informed Commander Ingraham, in reply, that he was altogether dependent on the Austrian
consul respecting Koszta. On the 29th, at daybreak, the St. Louis got under way, and anchored ahead of the Austrian brig. On the same day I received a letter from the legation, under date 27th June, in answer to mine
of the 24th, requesting me to continue my officious aid and intercession in
behalf of M. Koszta, informing me that the legation had applied to the Austrian minister for his immediate release. On receipt of this letter, I went
on board the St. Louis and communicated its contents to Commander Ingraham. During my interview with him as to the means to be adopted in behalf of Koszta, one of the officers of the corvette entered the cabin and told
the commander that the Austrians were loading their guns. Commander
Ingraham then gave orders to load the guns of the St. Louis. Commander
Ingraham and I decided that I should go to the Austrian consul and endeavor
to effect the release of Koszta, or that he should at least be kept here until
we should hear further from the legation of the result of its letter to the
Austrian minister. I therefore called on the Austrian consul, and my efforts for his release having proved unavailing, I then requested that he
should be kept here until further instructions from Constantinople. He at
first told me that he could not comply with my wishes, having received orders to send Koszta by the Steamer that was to leave on that day for Trieste.
Under these circumstances, I suggested the propriety of his keeping Koszta
here at least for eight days, but he refused to grant my desire, and it was
only after much opposition on his part that I was enabled to obtain a promise that he should not be sent away before Saturday, the 2d instant.

The steamer that came in on the 2d instant, from Constantinople,
brought me a letter from the legation, under date of the 30th ultimo, which
was handed me by one of its officers, who was sent here by the legation for
that purpose, wherein Mr. J.P. Brown, charge d'affaires, intimates that
Koszta might be released on the grounds that he had renounced all allegiance to Austria, and taken an oath of allegiance to the United States, and
that Commander Ingraham and I should have another interview with Koszta;
"and on any remark from him, calling for your protection, take him." On
receipt of this letter, I immediately went on board of the St. Louis to inform
Commander Ingraham of its contents, and to deliver a letter that Mr. Brown
had enclosed to the commander's address, under date 28th ultimo, requesting him to allow me to peruse it, wherein Mr. Brown says: "If I thought you
would be governed by my instructions, they would be to demand him (Koszta)
in the most formal and positive language of the Austrian commander, in
my name, as representative of the United States;" and adds, "in case of a
refusal to deliver him, founded on the please that he had renounced all allegiance to Austria, and that, having taken the oath of allegiance to the United
States, he has a claim upon our protection, I would take him out of the vessel." After a short consultation with Commander Ingraham, we agreed that
he should go on board, and see if Koszta called for American protection.
On his return, he informed me that when on board the brig he had demanded

Koszta's release, and had given the Austrian commander three hours' delay for effecting it -- (till 11 o'clock a.m.)

As I considered this delay not sufficient to take the necessary steps under the circumstances, I suggested to Commander Ingraham the propriety of extending it till 4 p.m., trusting that I might be enabled to come to some satisfactory understanding with the Austrian consul, so as to avoid the effusion of blood, and all the other consequences that might have ensued from an attempt to obtain Koszta's release by force. Commander Ingraham consented to my suggestions, and wrote a letter to the commander of the Austrian brig, demanding Koszta's release by 4 o'clock p.m. I took a copy of Commander Ingraham's letter and went to the Austrian consul, with whom I used all my efforts, so that Commander Ingraham's demand should be complied with; but after a very long debate, the Austrian consul positively refused to release Koszta. I then explained to him fully the consequences that would no doubt result from his refusal, upon which he proposed that Koszta should be kept here on board of the brig "for a week, a month, or even a year," until the question should be settled by the United States legation and the Austrian embassy at Constantinople. I took advantage of this opening to enter into negotiations, and after many difficulties I succeeded in making a convention with the Austrian consul, subject to Commander Ingraham's approval, whereby it is stipulated that Koszta is to be delivered to the French consul of this place, who is not to give him up until a collective demand is made by us to that effect.

Commander Ingraham having approved of the conditions therein stipulated, Martin Koszta was landed on the afternoon of the same day.

The excitement caused in town, among the European population and the natives, was very great. He was landed amidst the acclamation of an immense concourse of people, who went to see the man who had been rescued from Austrian barbarity, and cheers of "Vive l''Independence des Etats Unis d'Amerique, and her gallant commander who had saved the intended victim from the blood-thirsty Austrians," were long repeated by all present.

The governor of this place, "Ali Pacha," sent his dragoman to express the satisfaction he had felt on Koszta's release.

No measures of interference were taken by the local authorities in this matter, and the other authorities felt highly pleased at the happy result.

The firmness with which Commander Ingraham acted, under the circumstances, has greatly elevated the character of our country and its navy, especially as the Austrian force here was greatly superior to ours, as, besides the Austrian brig, there was a schooner of war and three Lloyd steamers, two of which were mounted with four guns each, and the third with eight, that had been sent on board from the brig the same morning.

I have the honor to enclose copies of the documents referring to this matter, and to transmit a despatch to the address of your excellency, with its enclosures, sent me by the United States legation at Constantinople, which Mr. Brown authorized me to peruse and forward by first mail.

With great respect and consideration, I remain, sir, your most obedient servant,

Hon. William L. Marcy   E.S. OFFLEY.
    Secretary of State, Washington

HUNGARIAN AMERICANS FIGHTING IN THE CIVIL WAR

Source: United States. Congress. House. Miscellaneous Documents. (52d Congress, 2d Session)

Report of Maj. Charles Zagonyi, Fremont's Body-Guard.

SPRINGFIELD, October 28, 1861
SIR: According to the order of Major-General Fremont, I left the
camp south of Pomme de Terre River on Thursday, the 24th instant, at
8.30 p.m., and proceeded towards Springfield. About 8 miles from that
place I captured five men belonging to picket guard and foraging parties.
A sixth escaped and gave the alarm to the rebels. I reached Springfield,
a distance of 51 miles, at 3 p.m. on the 25th. Knowing that the enemy was
apprised of our coming, I made a detour of 5 miles, to attack from another
side; but instead of finding the enemy in their old camp, I came suddenly
upon them, drawn up in line of battle, as I emerged from a wood near the
Mount Vernon road. The place was too confined for me to form my men.
I had to pass 250 yards down a lane and take down a rail fence at the end of
it, form in their camp, and make the first charge. My men belonging to
the Body-Guard amounted to 150, and were exposed from the moment we
entered the lane to a murderous cross-fire. Our first charge was com-
pletely successful. Half of my command charged upon the infantry and the
remainder upon the cavalry, breaking their line at every point. The infantry retired into a thick wood, where it was impossible to follow them. The
cavalry fled in all directions through the town. I rallied, and charged
through the streets in all directions about twenty times, clearing the town
and neighborhood, returning at last to the court-house, where I raised the
flag of one of my companies, liberated the prisoners, and united my men,
which now amounted to 70, the rest being scattered or lost. As it was nearly
dark I retired, in order not to run the risk of sacrificing the remainder of
my men, who were exhausted with the labors of the march and the battle.
Twenty men, with a corporal, who were without horses took possession of
the town, collected the wounded and placed them in the hospital, picked up
the dead, ordered out the Home Guard, and preserved order throughout the
next day.
On the 27th, at 5 o'clock a.m., I arrived again in the city, and from
the statements of citizens, scouts, and prisoners (the latter being Union
soldiers placed in front of the enemy's ranks to be shot at), I ascertained
that the rebel strength, as arrayed to receive our first charge, was 2,100
men. They had concentrated all the forces in the city to receive us. From
the beginning to the end the Body-Guard behaved with the most unparalleled
bravery and coolness. I have seen battles and cavalry charges before, but

I never imagined that a body of men could endure and accomplish so much in the face of such a fearful disadvantage. At the cry of "Fremont and the Union, " which was raised at every charge, they dashed forward repeatedly in perfect order and with resistless energy. Many of my officers, non-commissioned officers, and privates had three or even four horses killed under them, capturing new ones from the enemy. I cannot mention any names without doing great injustice to my command. Many performed acts of heroism. Not one but did his whole duty.

Our loss is as follows:

Killed -- Corporals, 6; privates, 9. Wounded -- Officers, 4; non-commissioned officers, 7; privates, 16. Missing -- Sergeant, 1; Corporal 1, privates, 8. Total loss, 52.

The loss of the enemy in killed alone, from the statement of citizens, scouts, and prisoners, was at least 106. How many wounded have since died I have no means of knowing, as they removed them in the night with wagons. Twenty-three of their dead were buried by the Body-Guard. We took 27 prisoners, $4,040 in gold, and about 60 stand of arms. Inclosed I send you a detailed account of our loss, with names.

Major White's command left me at the beginning of the action and before my first charge, and I saw no more of them until the next day at 10 o'clock. Captain Naughton and Lieutenant Conolly, who followed part way down the lane, were both wounded, the latter mortally, whereupon their company turned and followed the other two in spite of the efforts of the sergeant. Major White himself was made a prisoner before the battle, and placed with others in the enemy's front rank, but escaped uninjured.

In conclusion, I beg to urge the necessity of new clothing, arms, and horses for my command. Forty-five horses are killed or unfitted for use. Uniforms, haversacks, and extra clothes carried in the haversacks are so riddled with bullets as to be useless. Revolvers are also seriously damaged by the enemy's bullets.

Very respectfully,

CHAS. ZAGONYI,
Commanding Body-Guard.

Col. J.H. Eaton, Acting Asst. Adjt. Gen. , Springfield.

DISPATCHES FROM ZAGONYI
1861

Two dispatches from Zagonyi, concerning the
Springfield raid, published by the order of
Major-General Fremont.

Source: United States. Congress. House.
Miscellaneous Documents. (52nd Congress,
2d Session)

HEADQUARTERS WESTERN DEPARTMENT
Yost's Station, Mo., October 26, 1861.

By order of the general commanding, the following dispatches from the
brave Major Zagonyi are published, that all may know how much of success
to the cause of the country may be accomplished by discipline and good conduct, viz:

EIGHT MILES FROM SPRINGFIELD,
October 25, 1861 -- 11.30 a.m.
GENERAL: The information on which I can rely is that Wednesday
evening 1,500 men came into Springfield, and that at present there are not
less than 1,800 or 1,900 men. I march forward, and will try what I can do.
At the same time I would be thankful if some re-enforcement could come
after me. Should I be successful, I need them for guard; should I be de-
feated, to have some troops to fall back with my worn-out command. I will
report shortly again.

With high respect,

CHAS. ZAGONYI,
Major, Commanding Body-Guard.
Major-General FREMONT, Commanding.

FIVE MILES OF BOLIVAR,
October 26, 1861 -- 1 a.m.
GENERAL: I report respectfully that yesterday afternoon at 4 o'clock
I met in Springfield about 2,000 or 2,200 of the rebels in their camp, formed
in line of battle. They gave me a very warm reception -- warmer than I expected. But your Guard, with one feeling, made a charge, and in less than 3
3 minutes the 2,000 or 2,200 men were perfectly routed by 150 men of the
Body-Guard. We cleared out the city perfectly of every rebel, and raised
the Union flag on the court-house. It getting too dark, I concluded to leave
the city, not being able to keep it with 150 men. Major White's men did not
participate in the charge.

Allow me, general, to make you acquainted with the behavior of the
soldiers and officers. I have seen charges, but such brilliant unanimity

and bravery I have never seen and did not expect it. Their war cry, "Fremont and the Union," borke forth as thunder. Our loss comparatively small. I expected to remain on the field with them all. I will write about particulars.

With the highest respect, your obedient servant,

CHAS. ZAGONYI,
Major, Commanding Body-Guard.

Major-General FREMONT.
By order of Major-General Fremont:

J.H. EATON,
Acting Assistant Adjutant-General.

LETTER FROM GEZA MIHALOTZY

A letter from Geza Mihalotzy, the organizer
of the Chicago volunteer group named the Lincoln Rifle Men, reporting the results of an expedition under his command.

Source: United States. Congress. House, Miscellaneous Documents, Vol. 5, 7. (51st Congress, 2d Session)

HDQRS. 24TH REGT. ILLINOIS VOL. INFANTRY,
Chattanooga, Tenn., January 24, 1864

GENERAL: I have the honor to submit the following report detailing
additional results of the expedition under my command of detachment Third
Brigade, First Division, Fourteenth Army Corps, to Harrison and Ooltewah;

On the 20th instant the following-named 4 deserters from the rebel
army came into our lines, whom I sent to Provost-Marshal-General Wiles
the same day: John L. Tanner, private, Sixteenth Tennessee Infantry; J.
C. Cantrell, private, Sixteenth Tennessee Infantry; T.J. Cantrell, private,
Sixteenth Tennessee Infantry, stationed 4 miles below Dalton; Wm. P. Wor-
ley, private, Thirty-fifth Tennessee Infantry, stationed at Tunnell Hill.
They came from Tunnel Hill and Dalton, and report the strength of the
rebel forces at those places respectively as follows: At Tunnel Hill; three
brigades of infantry and a large force of artillery; at Dalton, two divisions
of infantry.

On the 21st instant, the morning after receiving your dispatch, in obedience to orders, I proceeded with my command to Ooltewah, while I sent
my train to Chattanooga by the direct road. With the train in charge of
Lieutenant Hodges, Thirty-seventh Indiana Volunteers, I sent 3 citizen
prisoners from the neighborhood of Harrison (J.T. Gardenhire, J.A. Hun-
ter, and _____ Lyon) to Provost-Marshal-General Wiles, who are
charged with having aided rebel guerrillas.

On approaching the town of Ooltewah about 10 a.m. I encountered a
squad of rebel cavalry, some 60 men strong, who, however, precipitately
fled from my advance guard, and having no cavalry at my disposal I was
unable to pursue them. The intention of this force was to get into the rear
and thereby cut off the communication of the scouting party of 50 under
Capt. H.A. Sheldon, of First Wisconsin Volunteers, whom I had sent out
on the preceding day, as reported in my dispatch of January 20, 1864.

On my way to Ooltewah, at the house of Anthony Moore, I seized the
records of the county registrar's office, comprising the following: Eighteen

volumes of records of registrar's office, County of Hamilton; two volumes Laws of Tennessee, 1857-'59; one volume Code of Tennessee. The above volumes are at my headquarters, to be disposed of according to instructions.

At Ooltewah I arrested Miss S. Locke and Miss Barnet, who have already been delivered to Provost-Marshal-General Wiles, both of whom are charged with carrying contraband information to the rebel army.

Through the scouting expedition above mentioned I have obtained the following information: The rebel forces at Tunnel Hill and Dalton, whose exact strength I was unable to ascertain, were reported doing considerable moving and shifting recently, the object of which, however, could not be learned. A force of 300 of Wheeler's rebel cavalry are encamped 5 miles beyond Igou's Gap, whose pickets are stationed at the gap. This force is continually making raids in small detachments on the Union towns and farms of that neighborhood, and committing all manner of outrages and cruelties on the loyal population. As an incident illustrative of the barbarities constantly being perpetrated by these outlaws, I will mention that a Mr. Tallent, a loyal citizen living near the forks of the roads leading to Red Clay and McDaniel's Gap, recently found in his immediate neighborhood a young child in a perishing condition, stripped of all its clothing, which the rebels had left there, having attempted by that means to find the father of the said child, whom they proposed to hang, he being a loyal citizen.

I have been reliably informed that a rebel raid on our river transportation at Harrison is now positively being prepared. This raiding force will have to pass through the mountain gaps near Ooltewah. The rebels infesting that region of country have been in the habit of disguising themselves in Federal uniforms, and have by this means often succeeded in deceiving the Union people. Messrs. Stone and Scroggins, Union citizens living at Julien's Gap, can give information of a guerrilla band commanded by a citizen of Ooltewah, who steal and plunder from the loyal citizens continually. They also know where a large portion of the spoils of this band are now secreted. A number of discharged soldiers from Tennessee regiments have banded together with Union citizens and organized themselves for self-defense. They are armed with such weapons as they have been able to procure, consisting of rifles, carbines, and revolvers. This band of loyal men, who are men of the highest sense of honor and true patriotism, are doing all they can to promote the success of our cause. Their number could be increased to 200 if arms could be provided for them. By their aid Surgeon Hung, of the Ninth Tennessee Infantry, whom I previously reported captured by guerrillas, was enabled to escape, and he is now in safety. I have also learned that the following named citizens, living in the vicinity of Ooltewah, are in the habit of harboring the guerrillas infesting that region, and that the rebels have signified their intention to burn the town of Ooltewah as soon as the families of the Misses Locke and Barnet, above mentioned, quit the town. After obtaining the above information from my scouting party, who returned about two hours after I arrived at Ooltewah, I took up the march to Chattanooga and arrived in camp at 9:30 o'clock the same day with my command, without having sustained any loss.

In conclusion I would again most respectfully beg leave to call the attention of the general commanding to the advantages to be gained by permanently stationing a small force at the town of Ooltewah. A force of two regiments with a half battery of artillery could, in conjunction with the organization of citizens above mentioned, hold all the mount passes in that region, thereby effectually preventing all raids, securing our river transportation, and affording to the almost exclusively loyal population the protection which they so much deserve. A great amount of most valuable information could also be obtained by such a force with the aid of the citizens of the band previously mentioned, they being intimately acquainted with the country thereabouts and able and willing to put in operation a most effective system of espionage for that purpose.

I have the honor to be, general, very respectfully, your most obedient servant,

G. MIHALOTZY,
Colonel 24th Regt. Ill. Vol. Inf., Commanding Expedition.
Maj. Gen. J.M. Palmer,
Commanding Fourteenth Corps.
[Indorsement]
HDQRS. FOURTEENTH ARMY CORPS,
Chattanooga, January 24, 1864

Respectfully forwarded, and attention called to the highly judicious suggestions of Colonel Mihalotzy.

J.M. PALMER,
Major-General, Commanding.

Fort named after Colonel Geza Mihalotzy.

GENERAL ORDERS   HDQRS. DEPT. OF THE CUMBERLAND,
No. 63.   Chattanooga, Tenn., April 27, 1864

10. The fort on the spur of Cameron Hill, immediately south of the gap and of the summit of the hill, will be called Fort Mihalotzy, in honor of Col. Geza Mihalotzy, Twenty-fourth Regiment Illinois Volunteers, who was killed in the affair before Dalton, February 25, 1864.

WM. D. WHIPPLE,
Assistant Adjutant-General

THEODORE ROOSEVELT AND THE HUNGARIANS

Source: Antoinette Feleky, Charles Feleky
and His Unpublished Manuscript, New York:
Representative Press, 1938.

Extract from President Theodore Roosevelt's address delivered at the
dinner of "The Hungarian Republican Club" May 31, 1899, when he was
Governor of New York State.

"If you bring into American life the spirit of the heroes of Hungary,
you have done your share. There is nothing this country needs more than
that there shall be put before its men and its future men -- its boys; and
its girls, too -- the story of such lives as that of Kossuth. . . . "

Extract from President Theodore Roosevelt's address delivered at the
dinner of "The Hungarian Republican Club" February 14th 1905.

"Americanism is not a matter of birthplace, of ancestry, of creed, of
occupation: Americanism is a matter of the spirit that is within a man's
soul.   From the time when we first became an independent nation to the
present moment there has never been a generation in which some of the
most distinguished and most useful men were not men who had been born
on the other side of the Atlantic; and it is peculiarly appropriate and to me
peculiarly pleasant that in addressing this Club of the men upon whose efforts so much of the future welfare of this city, of this State, of this Nation,
depends I should be addressing men who show by their actions that they
know no difference between Jew and Gentile, Catholic and Protestant, native
born and foreign born; provided only the man, whatever his creed, whatever his birthplace strives to live so as to do his full duty by his neighbor
and by the country as a whole."

DOCUMENTS RELATING TO THE HUNGARIAN REVOLUTION OF 1956

1. Expressing the Sense of the Congress on the Problem of Hungary

2. Emigration of Refugees and Escapees

3. Recording the Admission of Certain Hungarian Refugees

Source: (1) United States. Congress. House of Representatives. Report No. 1023. (85th Congress, 1st Session). (2) United States. Congress. Senate. Report No. 129. (85th Congress, 1st Session). (3) United States. Congress. House of Representatives. Report No. 1661. (85th Congress, 2nd Session).

EXPRESSING THE SENSE OF THE CONGRESS ON THE PROBLEM OF HUNGARY

AUGUST 6, 1957.—Ordered to be printed

Mrs. KELLY of New York, from the committee of conference, submitted the following

CONFERENCE REPORT

[To accompany H. Con. Res. 204]

The committee of conference on the disagreeing votes of the two Houses on the amendments of the Senate to the concurrent resolution (H. Con. Res. 204) expressing the sense of the Congress on the problem of Hungary, having met, after full and free conference, have agreed to recommend and do recommend to their respective Houses as follows:

That the House recede from its disagreement to the amendment of the Senate to the text of the resolution and agree to the same with an amendment as follows:

In lieu of the matter proposed to be inserted by the Senate amendment insert the following: *That it is the sense of the Congress that the President, through the United States representatives to the United Nations at the forthcoming special reconvening of the General Assembly of the United Nations, should take every appropriate action toward the immediate consideration and adoption of the report of the United Nations Special Committee on the Problem of Hungary and toward the immediate consideration of other available information on the brutal action of the Soviet Union in Hungary. It is further the sense of the Congress that the President, through such United States representatives, should at such reconvened session join actively in seeking the most effective way of dealing with the report of the United Nations Special Committee in order to advance the objectives of the United Nations regarding the situation in Hungary, to prevent further repressive action by the Soviet Union, and to seek all practical redress of the wrong which has been committed in violation of the principles of the United Nations and the elemental requirements of humanity.*

SEC. 2. *It is the sense of the Congress that the United States should implement policies, through the United Nations or in cooperation with the peoples of the free world, that will work toward the freedom and independence of the captive nations, and will effectively utilize the position of the United States through all proper means, to the end that the Hungarian tragedy shall not be repeated anywhere.*

And the Senate agree to the same.

That the House recede from its disagreement to the amendment of the Senate to the preamble of the resolution and agree to the same with an amendment as follows:

In lieu of the matter proposed to be inserted by the Senate amendment insert the following:

Whereas the Hungarian freedom revolution which broke out October 23, 1956, was catastrophic in nature, and subsequent events shocked the conscience of the free peoples of the world; and

Whereas the barbaric action of the Soviet Union in Hungary demonstrates that the Soviet Union is determined to go to any and all lengths to maintain its empire of enslaved peoples by the most brutal forms of armed subjugation and repression; and

Whereas the Special Committee on the Problem of Hungary, created by the General Assembly of the United Nations under its resolution 1132 (XI) adopted at its six hundred and thirty-sixth plenary meeting on January 10, 1957, has established that what took place in Hungary in the latter part of 1956 was a spontaneous national uprising caused by long-standing grievances engendered by the oppressive way of life under Communist rule and by the state of captivity of Hungary under control of the Union of Soviet Socialist Republics; and

Whereas the crisis and foment created by developments in the satellite nations require a continued reevaluation by the United States and the United Nations of strategic policy to meet changing conditions: Now, therefore, be it

Senate agree to the same.

EDNA F. KELLY,
WAYNE L. HAYS,
ARMISTEAD I. SELDEN, Jr.,
JAMES G. FULTON,
Managers on the Part of the House.
THEODORE FRANCIS GREEN,
WILLIAM F. KNOWLAND,
Managers on the Part of the Senate.

EMIGRATION OF REFUGEES AND ESCAPEES

MARCH 4 (legislative day, MARCH 2), 1957.—Ordered to be printed

Mr. EASTLAND (for Mr. LANGER), from the Committee on the Judiciary, submitted the following

REPORT

[Pursuant to S. Res. 168, 84th Cong., 2d sess., as extended by S. Res. 84, 85th Cong.]

As to the Hungarian situation, it is estimated that during the period from October through December 1956, 154,000 Hungarians fled to Austria. The Austrian Government and the Austrian people have been most generous to the Hungarians. Many thousands of Austrian citizens have taken the Hungarians into their homes to live temporarily. The Austrian economy is taxed to the limit and it is recognized that such a drain cannot continue indefinitely. President Eisenhower took cognizance of this fact when he sent his message of January 31, 1957, to the Congress, which is as follows:

THE WHITE HOUSE

To the Congress of the United States:

The eyes of the free world have been fixed on Hungary over the past 2½ months. Thousands of men, women, and children have fled their homes to escape Communist oppression. They seek asylum in countries that are free. Their opposition to Communist tyranny is evidence of a growing resistance throughout the world. Our position of world leadership demands that, in partnership with the other nations of the free world, we be in a position to grant that asylum.

Moreover, in the 4½ years that have elapsed since the enactment of the Immigration and Nationality Act, the practical application of that law has demonstrated certain provisions which operate inequitably and others which are outmoded in the world of today.

Prompt action by the Congress is needed looking toward the revision and improvement of that law.

Last October the people of Hungary, spontaneously and against tremendous odds, rose in revolt against Communist domination. When it became apparent that they would be faced with ruthless deportation or extinction, a mass exodus into Austria began. Fleeing for their lives, tens of thousands crossed the border into Austria seeking asylum. Austria, despite its own substantial economic problems, unselfishly and without hesitation received these destitute refugees. More than 20 nations have expressed their willingness to accept large numbers of them.

On November 8, I directed that extraordinary measures be taken to expedite the processing of 5,000 Hungarian visa applications under the provisions of the Refugee Relief Act. On November 19, the first of this group departed from Vienna for the United States. By November 29, it had become clear that the flight of Hungarian men, women, and children to gain freedom was assuming major proportions.

On December 1, I directed that above and beyond the available visas under the Refugee Relief Act—approximately 6,500 in all—emergency admission should be granted to 15,000 additional Hungarians through the exercise by the Attorney General of his discretionary authority under section 212 (d) (5) of the Immigration and Nationality Act; and that when these numbers had been exhausted, the situation be reexamined.

On December 12, I requested the Vice President to go to Austria so that he might inspect, first hand, the tragic situation which faced the refugees. I also appointed a President's Committee for Hungarian Refugee Relief to assure full coordination of the work of the voluntary agencies with each other and with the various Government agencies involved.

On January 1, 1957, following his return to the United States, the Vice President made a personal inspection of our reception center at Camp Kilmer and then reported to me his findings and recommendations. He reported that the people who had fled from Hungary were largely those who had been in the forefront of the fight for freedom. He concluded that "the countries which accept these refugees will find that, rather than having assumed a liability, they have acquired a valuable national asset."

Most of the refugees who have come to the United States have been admitted only temporarily on an emergency basis. Some may ultimately decide that they should settle abroad. But many will wish to remain in the United States permanently. Their admission to the United States as parolees, however, does not permit permanent residence or the acquisition of citizenship. I believe they should be given that opportunity under a law which deals both with the current escapee problem and with any other like emergency which may hereafter face the free world.

First, I recommend that the Congress enact legislation giving the President power to authorize the Attorney General to parole into the United States temporarily under such conditions as he may prescribe escapees, selected by the Secretary of State, who have fled or in the future flee from Communist persecution and tyranny. The number to whom such parole may be granted should not exceed in any one year the average number of aliens who, over the past 8 years, have been permitted to enter the United States by special acts of Congress outside the basic immigration system.

Second, I urge the Congress promptly to enact legislation giving the necessary discretionary power to the Attorney General to permit aliens paroled into the United States, who intend to stay here, to remain as permanent residents. Consistent with existing procedures, provision should be made for submission of the cases to Congress so that no alien will become a permanent resident if it appears to the Congress that permanent residence in his case is inappropriate. Legislation of this type would effectively solve the problem of the Hungarian escapees who have already arrived, and furthermore would provide a means for coping with the cases of certain Korean orphans, adopted children, and other aliens who have been granted emergency admission to this country and now remain here in an indefinite status. This should be permanent legislation so that administrative authorities are in a position to act promptly and with assurance in facing emergencies which may arise in the future.

RECORDING THE ADMISSION OF CERTAIN HUNGARIAN REFUGEES

APRIL 28, 1958.—Committed to the Committee of the Whole House on the State of the Union and ordered to be printed

Mr. WALTER, from the Committee on the Judiciary, submitted the following

REPORT

[To accompany H. R. 11033]

The Committee on the Judiciary, to whom was referred the bill (H. R. 11033) to authorize the creation of record of admission for permanent residence in the case of certain Hungarian refugees, having considered the same, report favorably thereon with amendment and recommend that the bill do pass.

The amendment is as follows:

On page 2, line 6, after the words "at the time of", insert the word "his".

PURPOSE OF THE BILL

The purpose of the bill is to provide for the retroactive adjustment of the immigration status of Hungarian refugees who were paroled into the United States subsequent to October 23, 1956, if they are found to be qualified for admission under all the requirements of the Immigration and Nationality Act other than a lack of the documents specified in section 212 (a) (20) of that act. The bill provides for the inspection under applicable procedural requirements of all such aliens who have been in the United States for at least 2 years and preserves intact the Attorney General's parole authority. The committee amendment is technical in nature and does not affect the purpose of the bill.

EXECUTIVE RECOMMENDATION AND REPORT

The following communication from the Attorney General, transmitting the final report of the Commissioner of Immigration and Naturalization on the Hungarian escapee program, was addressed to the chairman of the committee on February 15, 1958:

FEBRUARY 15, 1958.

Hon. EMANUEL CELLER,
    Chairman, Committee on the Judiciary,
        House of Representatives, Washington, D. C.
    DEAR MR. CHAIRMAN: I am transmitting for your information the final report of the Immigration and Naturalization Service, with the accompanying letter of Commissioner Joseph M. Swing, on the operation of the Hungarian-escapee program of the United States which terminated on December 31, 1957.

The report shows the Immigration and Naturalization Service has carried out this massive and unprecedented operation on behalf of the Department of Justice efficiently, expeditiously, and with compassion for the individual and concern for our Nation's welfare and security. I believe all Americans can be very proud of the enormous contribution thus made to the advancement of their country and the rest of the free world in the continuing struggle against Communist tyranny.

The one remaining step to bring the escapee program to a successful conclusion now falls to the Congress—the enactment of legislation to authorize permanent resident status for deserving Hungarians who were admitted to the United States under the program by parole. These Hungarians, unlike those fortunate few granted asylum under the provisions of the expiring Refugee Relief Act, have neither the privileges nor the security of permanent residents. Unless they can adjust their status to become permanent residents, they can never seek to become citizens. Certainly our responsibilities to them and to the free world require that they should be permitted to look forward to the day when, after they have lived uprightly in the United States for a definite period, the temporary asylum they have sought so fearfully will become their home.

As you know, H. R. 4202 and H. R. 4205, identical general immigration measures, are pending with your committee. Section 5 of these bills contains provisions for the adjustment of status of paroled Hungarians which would accomplish the desired objective. I earnestly hope that the enclosed report will serve to stimulate renewed interest in the pending legislation and that your committee will take early favorable action.
    Sincerely yours,

WILLIAM P. ROGERS,
    Attorney General.

MY DEAR MR. ATTORNEY GENERAL: There is submitted herewith the final report of Immigration and Naturalization Service operations in the Hungarian escapee program of the United States which terminated on December 31, 1957.

The story of the aborted revolt of the Hungarian peoples against

their own and foreign oppressors and the accounts of the flight of
these patriots to Austria and Yugoslavia have been well and fully
reported elsewhere.

On November 8, 1956, the President of the United States announced
that 5,000 escapees would be accepted into the United States as our
contribution to the cooperative efforts of the governments of the
Western World both to aid the freedom fighters and to ease the burden
on Austria, whose resources were inadequate to house, clothe, and
feed the refugees.

Officers of this Service stationed at the consulates in Germany,
Italy, and the Netherlands were detailed immediately to Austria to
assist in the programs to carry out the President's purpose. The
balance of special nonquota immigration visas under section 4 (a) (2)
of the Refugee Relief Act were allocated by the Department of State
to the Hungarian escapees in Austria. The first visa was issued on
November 19, 1956, and the first planeload of visaed immigrants left
Austria on November 20, arriving at Maguire Air Force Base in
New Jersey on the following day. By December 1 the last of the
6,130 available numbers had been assigned. On that date there
remained in Austria, despite the removal of 38,000 of the first arrivals
to other countries, approximately 75,000 fugitives. Their number
was being increased by an average of 2,000 daily crossings of the
Hungarian-Austrian border.

On the instructions of your predecessor I had arrived in Vienna on
November 19, 1956, in the company of the chairman of the Immigration Subcommittee of the House Committee on the Judiciary, Mr.
Francis Walter of Pennsylvania. My observations on the general
conditions in Austria, following surveys at the border and in the
refugee camps of that country, and the operations of the international
organizations, and the public and private agencies of the United States
were orally reported to Mr. Brownell on my return, with my recommendation for an expanded program.

Pursuant to the directive of the Attorney General, implementing
the President's announcement that an additional 15,000 Hungarian
escapees would be offered asylum in this country, I invoked the
authority delegated to me under section 212 (d) (5) of the Immigration
and Nationality Act and authorized the entry of that number to the
United States as parolees. The responsibility of examination and
selection of applicants for admission to the United States thereafter
was the exclusive responsibility of this Service.

The immigration officer force in Vienna and Salzburg was augmented
by additional officers detailed from the United States, two of whom
were Hungarian-speaking officers, one born in Budapest, the other of
Hungarian extraction. Their first task was to investigate the com-
petence and reliability of interpreters and other locally employed
clerical assistants. Because of chaotic conditions of transport and
communication, the absence of a central registry of refugees, and the
size of our force (at no time did the number of Immigration officers
exceed 17), representatives of the private United States voluntary
agencies were authorized to distribute and assist in the preparation
of specially designed application forms and to present for examination
daily an assigned quota of applicants.

The broad eligibility requirements were flight from Hungary after
October 23, 1956, and admissibility to the United States under the
provisions of the general immigration laws. A single exception was

made in behalf of 300 accompanying members of otherwise admissible family units who were afflicted with tuberculosis. This was the first time in the post-World War II refugee programs of the United States that such afflicted persons were authorized to enter the United States and further established our intention to welcome a representative cross section of the escapees in Austria. In passing it should be noted that the first session of this Congress incorporated this policy in the basic immigration law of the United States.

During January 1957, through the cooperation of the Austrian authorities, application forms were made available throughout that country to every Hungarian national who desired to be considered for migration to the United States. The applications were cataloged by date of entry into Austria and relationship, if any, to persons in the United States. From this central registry, maintained in our Vienna office, applicants were thereafter selected by the Service and given appointments for interview. No attempt was made to substitute the opinion of any stateside official of this Service for the judgment of the officer in charge at Vienna in weighing the numerous intangibles which governed the selection of candidates for interview. The United States voluntary agencies agreed to continue their assistance in locating employment and housing in the United States for the vast majority who did not have individual sponsors. They also assumed major responsibility for locating and transporting to the examination centers in Vienna and Salzburg those escapees selected for interview.

In May 1957 parole examination was extended to other western European countries for the purpose of reuniting in the United States members of the immediate families of Hungarian escapees who had become separated in the flight to Austria or during the early removals from that country. A total of 517 such persons were selected in 15 "countries of second asylum."

In July 1957, following a survey in Yugoslavia and consultations with officials of that country, parole operations were extended to cover Hungarian escapees who had fled directly into Yugoslavia and who were being cared for in refugee camps operated by that Government. Of 3,451 applicants who were interviewed, 2,416 were passed for parole.

Examination of all parole applicants consisted of the identical medical examination, including X-rays by physicians of the United States Public Health Service as is accorded normal immigration visa applicants, and interrogation and fingerprinting of each principal applicant and accompanying member of his family over the age of 14 by United States immigration officers. The records of the established security and intelligence agencies of this Government were examined. Lookout lists of the Budapest and Vienna consulates were checked and maximum use was made of informants among the refugees whose general desire to purge their own ranks of undesirables can well be appreciated.

With the close of the program it is now appropriate to reveal that the Service is in possession of a thoroughly authenticated copy of an official listing of principal functionaires of the Hungarian Communist Party at all levels, against which all applicants for parole were also checked.

The within-Europe transportation of parolees was arranged by the Intergovernmental Committee for European Migration and the transatlantic transportation was handled under the auspices of that organization but for the most part on planes and vessels of the Military Air Transport and Military Sea Transport Services.

The general operation of the Army-reactivated reception center at Camp Kilmer, N. J., has been described in the report of Mr. Tracy Vorhees, Chairman of the President's Committee on Hungarian Refugees. A brief description of Service operations there suffices for this report.

All normal public health, customs, and immigration inspection usually performed at the time and place of actual United States entry was deferred to Camp Kilmer. Each refugee was photographed and, following the authorization of parole, each was issued a laminated "parole identification card." No refugee was released from the camp until the officer in charge of the Service was satisfied that the subject and the members of his family had confirmed housing and employment or assurances of support.

On May 1, 1957, after 31,869 refugees had arrived at Kilmer, the need for such a large installation having ceased, future reception operations were transferred to Service-operated quarters in the St. George Hotel, Brooklyn, N. Y., for the remainder of the program.

The investigation of the parolees did not cease with their entry into the United States. All allegations of a derogatory nature received from any source are thoroughly investigated. Over 3,000 such investigations have been completed, resulting in a total parole revocation and return to Austria of 74 principal parolees and 43 accompanying members of their families.

In accordance with assurances given Hungarian refugees that this Government would assist those who, after arrival in the United States, desired to return to Hungary, a total of 290 voluntary repatriates have been returned to Austria for transit to Hungary, after it has been determined that each individual has made his decision freely and without fear or threat. No refugee has been returned to Hungary against his will.

The attached statistical tables reflect the total movements of Hungarians from Austria by all cooperating governments (and the total of emigrants from each such country to the United States under normal immigration), the age, sex, and major occupational groupings of the 31,738 parolees who had entered the United States by the close of business on December 31, 1957, and an analysis of rejected cases in all areas.

The processing of this mass migration, probably without comparison in our history, was effected with dispatch and yet without sacrifice of our national standards. The attached factual tables establish beyond a doubt the potential value to the United States of the Hungarians who came to this country since the October 1956 revolt. As a final demonstration of our national good faith, and to complete the special Hungarian program, there remains only the enactment of legislation to provide a method for authorizing permanent resident status for those Hungarians who have entered as parolees.

    Sincerely,

                J. M. SWING,
Commissioner of Immigration and Naturalization.

RECORD ADMISSION OF CERTAIN HUNGARIAN REFUGEES

Intergovernmental Committee for European Migration: Hungarian refugee situaiton, Austria, Dec. 31, 1957

1. Breakdown of departures by country of destination:
   (a) Overseas:

Argentina	906
Australia	9, 423
Brazil	977
Canada	24, 525
Chile	258
Colombia	215
Costa Rica	15
Cuba	5
Dominican Republic	581
Ecuador	1
Rhodesia	40
Israel	1, 893
New Zealand	960
Nicaragua	4
Paraguay	7
Turkey	505
Union of South Africa	1, 309
Uruguay	35
Venezuela	549
United States of America	35, 026

   (b) Within Europe:

Belgium	3, 416
Cyprus	2
Denmark	1, 173
France	10, 232
Germany	14, 270
Iceland	52
Ireland	541
Italy	3, 849
Luxembourg	227
Netherlands	3, 556
Norway	1, 159
Portugal	4
Spain	19
Sweden	5, 453
Switzerland	11, 962
United Kingdom	20, 590

2. Residing in Austria ... 18, 993

Total ... 172, 732

HUNGARIAN RECIPIENTS OF THE MEDAL OF HONOR
IN THE UNITED STATES

Source: Medal of Honor Recipients 1863-
1973. Washington, U.S. Government Printing Office, 1973. (93d Congress 1st Session.)

MOLNAR, FRANKIE ZOLY

Rank and organization: Staff Sergeant, United States Army, Company
B, 1st Battalion, 8th Infantry, 4th Infantry Division. Place and date: Kontum Province, Republic of Vietnam, 20 May 1967. Entered service at:
Fresno, Calif. Date and place of birth: February 14, 1943, Logan, W.
Va. Citation: For conspicuous gallantry and intrepidity in action at the
risk of his life above and beyond the call of duty. Sergeant Molnar distinguished himself while serving as a squad leader with Company B, 1st
Battalion, 8th Infantry, 4th Infantry Division, on 20 May 1967 during com-
bat operations in Kontum Province, Republic of Vietnam. Shortly after
the battalion's defensive perimeter was established, it was hit by intense
mortar fire as the prelude to a massive enemy night attack. Sergeant
Molnar immediately left his sheltered location to insure the readiness of
his squad to meet the attack. As he crawled through the position, he discovered a group of enemy soldiers closing in on his squad area. His
accurate rifle fire killed five of the enemy and forced the remainder to
flee. When the mortar fire stopped, the enemy attacked in a human wave
supported by grenades, rockets, automatic weapons, and small arms
fire. After assisting to repel the first enemy assault, Sergeant Molnar
found that his squad's ammunition and grenade supply was nearly expended.
Again leaving the relative safety of his position, he crawled through intense enemy fire to secure additional ammunition and distribute it to his
squad. He rejoined his men to beat back the renewed enemy onslaught,
and he moved about his area providing medical aid and assisting in the
evacuation of the wounded. With the help of several men, he was prepar-
ing to move a severely wounded soldier when an enemy handgrenade was
thrown into the group. The first to see the grenade, Sergeant Molnar
threw himself on it and absorbed the deadly blast to save his comrades.
His demonstrated selflessness and inspirational leadership on the battlefield were a major factor in the successful defense of the American position and are in keeping with the finest traditions of the United States Army.
Sergeant Molnar's actions reflect great credit upon himself, his unit, and
the United States Army.

RABEL, LASZLO

Rank and organization: Staff Sergeant, United States Army, 74th

Infantry Detachment, (Long Range Patrol), 173rd Airborne Brigade. Place
and date: Binh Dinh Province, Republic of Vietnam, 13 November 1968.
Entered service at: Minneapolis, Minn. Date and place of birth: September
21, 1939, Budapest, Hungary. Citation: For conspicuous gallantry and
intrepidity in action at the risk of his life above and beyond the call of
duty. Staff Sergeant Laszlo Rabel distinguished himself by conspicuous
gallantry and intrepidity while serving as leader of Team Delta, 74th
Infantry Detachment (Long Range Patrol), 173rd Airborne Brigade in Binh
Dinh Province, Republic of Vietnam on 13 November 1968. At 1000 hours
on this date, Team Delta was in a defensive perimeter conducting recon-
naissance of enemy trail networks when a member of the team detected
enemy movement to the front. As Sergeant Rabel and a comrade prepared
to clear the area, he heard an incoming grenade as it landed in the midst
of the team's perimeter. With complete disregard for his own life, Sergeant Rabel threw himself on the grenade and, covering it with his body,
received the complete impact of the immediate explosion. Through his
indomitable courage, complete disregard for his own safety and profound
concern for his fellow soldiers, Sergeant Rabel averted the loss of life
and injury to the other members of Team Delta. By his conspicuous gallantry at the cost of his own life in the highest traditions of the military
service, Staff Sergeant Rabel has reflected great credit upon himself, his
unit, and the United States Army.

TABOR, WILLIAM L.S.
    Rank and Organization: Private, Company K, 15th New Hampshire
Infantry. Place and Date: At the siege of Port Hudson, La., July 1863.
Entered Service at: --------. Birth: --------. Date of Issue: 10 Mar.
1896. Citation: Voluntarily exposed himself to the enemy only a few feet
away to render valuable services for the protection of his comrades.

STAHEL, JULIUS
    Rank and Organization: Major General, United States Volunteers.
Place and Date: At Piedmont, Va., 5 June 1864. Entered Service at: -----.
Birth: Hungary. Date of Issue: 4 Nov. 1893. Citation: Led his division into
action until he was severely wounded.

VADAS, ALBERT
    Rank and organization: Seaman, U.S. Navy. (Name changed to Wadas,
Albert.) Born: 26 March 1876, Austria-Hungary. Accredited to: New York.
G.O. No.: 521, 7 July 1899. Citation: On board the U.S.S. Marblehead
during the operation of cutting the cable leading from Cienfuegos, Cuba,
11 May 1898. Facing the heavy fire of the enemy, Vadas displayed extraordinary bravery and coolness throughout this period.

APPENDICES

I have already noted in the introduction that the following twelve appendices are intended to subserve the dual function of documentation and reference material. It may be worth repeating that these appendices offer, like the chronology, merely what I hope to be a representative cross-section of the data which I have examined or which I know of but have not had the opportunity to examine personally. For, as I hope the perusal of this volume even up to this point has made abundantly clear, the history of Hungarian-Americans -- or of the political, economic, and cultural contacts between the United States and Hungary -- is remarkably long and broad. An exhaustive listing with respect to any of the subjects covered in the appendices would be impossible even in greater space and time than were available for this work. Thus I have exercised editorial discretion by selecting what appeared to me noteworthy and representative entries.

PROMINENT HUNGARIANS IN AMERICA
PAST AND PRESENT

According to a comparative examination of the three editions of Hungarians in America, A Biographical Directory of Professionals of Hungarian Origin in the Americas, there are at present at least 9000 Hungarian professionals in the United States. Their total number is undoubtedly much higher, since I personally happen to know several dozens who are not included in this or any other directory of Hungarians or Hungarian-Americans only. It would be virtually impossible to track them down in directories in which they are listed together with persons of non-Hungarian origin (even if the ethnic origins of the persons listed were given).

FAMOUS HUNGARIAN-AMERICANS

Entertainment

Lorenzo Alváry, opera singer
Lorant Andahazy, ballet dancer
John Auer, producer & film director
Vilma Bánky, actress
Margaret Bokor, opera singer
Gábor Carelli, opera singer
Leslie Chabay, opera singer
George D. Cukor, film producer
Michael Curtis, film director
Tony Curtis, actor
Lili Darvas, actress
Dezsö Ernster, opera singer
Ella Flesch, opera singer
William Fox, film producer
Éva Gábor, actress
Zsa-zsa Gábor, actress
Miklós Gafni, opera singer
Sándor Kónya, opera singer
Zoltán Korda, producer & film director
Vincent Korda, producer & film director
Ernie Kovacs, actor
Nóra Kovács, ballet dancer
Albert Lichtman, financier and manager of film distribution
Peter Lorre, actor
Béla Lugosi, actor
Paul Lukas, actor
Alexander Markey, film executive producer
Ilona Massey, actress
George Pál, film producer
Gabriel Pascal, film producer and director
Joseph Pasternak, film producer and director
Antal Pager, actor
Steve Rabovszky, ballet dancer
Maria Samson, opera singer

Alexander Svéd, opera singer
Sándor Szabó, actor
Michael Székely, opera singer
Zita Szeleczky, actress
Éva Szörényi, actress
George Tatár, ballet dancer
Kate Tatár, ballet dancer
Iván Tors, film producer, director
Victor Varconi, actor
Cornel Wilde, actor
Adolph Zukor, film producer

Fine Arts

Theodor Bauman, painter
Kate Benedek, illustrator
Emile Bernát, tapestry
Julius Bethlen, sculptor
Lester J. Chaney, illustrator
Joseph Csillag, genre painter
Stephen Csóka, painter
John Csösz, painter
Alis Dersó, cartoonist
Steven Dohános, illustrator
Joseph Domján, wood-cut artist
Michel M. Engel, illustrator
John Ettle, sculptor
Alexandra Finta, sculptor
Lily Füredy, painter
Emery Gellért, painter
Hugo Gellért, painter
Laci de Gerenday, sculptor
Franz Geritz, painter
Jenö Gyimesy-Kasas, painter
Arthur Halmi, portrait painter
Bertha de Hellebranth, painter
Elene de Hellebranth, painter
Nicholas Hornyánszki, illustrator
Ferdinand H. Horváth, illustrator
Stephen Hospodar, painter
Charles Illawa, sculptor
Frank Imrey, mural painter

Lajos Jámbor, mural painter
Joseph Jakovits, painter, sculptor
Victor Jeney, portrait painter
Géza Juszkó, sculptor
Ilonka Karasz, illustrator
András Károly, mural painter
Alexander R. Katz, etching
Géza Káro, fresco painter
Pál Kelemen, art historian
Imre Kelen, cartoonist
György Kepes, painter
Alexander Keszthelyi, painter
Julio Kilényi, sculptor
Leo Kober, illustrator
Ernö Koch, fresco painter
Eugene Körmendi, sculptor
George Kósa, water colors
Henry Major, painter
Lajos Mark, portrait painter
Géza Maróti, sculptor
Laszló Moholy-Nagy, industrial designer
Martin Munkácsi, photographer
Andras Ösze, sculptor, painter
Duchess Vilma Parlaghy-Lwoff, portrait painter
Gábor Peterdy, artist, print
Willy Pogány, mural painter
Aurel Raskó, portrait painter
Steven Rettegi, portrait, landscape, and still life painter
Francis Révész-Ferryman, mural painter
Zoltán Sepeshy, painter
Sandor Vágó-Vayos, painter
Marcel Vértes, illustrator
Lajos Szalay, graphic artist (won Unesco prizes)
Lajos Szanto, mural painter
William Zolnay, sculptor

Industry, Business

Martin Benedek, President of the Automatic Manufacturing Corporation of New York

John Bosko, owned the Maffit Tool and Machine Company
Charles Buday, owner of a machine factory in Newark
Antal and Ferenc Chase, founders of the Chase Brothers Cabinet Makers, Inc., New York
Charles Eisler, owner of a tube manufacturing company in Newark
Charles L. Fleischmann, founder of the Standard Brands Yeast Factories
Heiser Brothers, owned the United Engineering firm at St. Louis
Daniel J. Hertz, founder of the Omnibus Corporation of America
Bela Koteles, founder of the Pemco factory in Cleveland
Jacques Kreisler, Chairman of the Board of Jacques Kreisler Manufacturing Company
Charles Nagy, owner of a paint factory in Chicago
Ladislas Páthy, owner of a world-wide shipping company in New York
Louis Szánthó, tobacco manufacturer in Virginia
Louis Szathmáry, writer, businessman, owner of the Bakery restaurant in Chicago
Hugo Urbauer, established a foundation at Washington University
Luis Weiss, owner of the Ideal Cooler of St. Louis

Literature

Tamás Aczél, writer
Zsolt Aradi, religious writer
Lajos Biró, film writer
Ida Bobula, essayist
Stephen Borsody, political writer
Tibor Eckhardt, political writer
Béla Fábián, political writer

Ferenc Faragó, film writer
Mary Fay, film writer
László Bús Fekete, film writer
Edna Ferber, writer (Pulitzer prize 1924)
Alexander Finta, writer
Tibor Flórián, poet
Eugene Fodor, editor, publisher, president of Fodor's Modern Guides, Inc.
Rene Fülöp-Miller, historical writer
Lajos Füry, writer
Astric Gabriel, historical writer
Joseph Grósz, translator
Hans Habe, writer
Michael Heilprin, encyclopaedist
Gezá Herczeg, film writer
Ignotus-Veingelsberg, essayist
Oscár Jászi, historical writer
Elizabeth Kaeburn, playwright
Miklós Kállay, political writer
Georg Kemény, poet
Frederick Kerenyi, poet
Stephan Kertész, political writer
Andor C. Klay, historical writer
Leslie Könnyü, writer, poet, researcher
Ferenc Körmendi, novelist
Belá Kornitzer, political writer
Imre Kovács, political writer
Cornel Lengyel, political writer
Emil Lengyel, historical writer
Melchior Lengyel, writer
Anna Lesznai, translator
Stephen Loránt, historical writer
János Lucas, political writer
Ádám Makkai, poet
Alexander Márai, writer
Gilbert Mihályi, political writer
Ferenc Molnár, writer
Ferenc Nagy, political writer
Anthony Nyerges, translator
Adorján Ötvös, film writer
Stephen Parmenius of Buda, poet, humanist (d. 1583)
Ferenc Pártos, film writer

Michael Petersham, writer
Joseph Pulitzer, journalist
Joseph Reményi, essayist, translator
Emery Reves, historical writer
Ernst Rickert, anthologist
Robert J. Rombauer, historian
Endre Sebestyén, writer, linguist
Kate Seredy, writer, illustrator (Newberry Medal, 1938)
Ferenc Somogyi, historical writer
Bélla Spewack, film writer
Theresa Stibran, writer
George Szecskay, poet
Ákos Tolnay, film writer
Charles de Tolnay, art historian, writer
Ernö Vajda, film writer
Steven Béla Várdy, historical writer
Ferenc Wágner, political writer
Albert Wass, writer, publisher
Lajos Zilahy, writer

Military and Public Service

Alexander Asbóth, Brigadier-General in the Civil War
Victor Berger, New York, first Socialist Congressman in the U.S. House of Representatives, 1911, 1923
Philip Figyelmessy, Inspector-General in the Civil War, American Consul in British Guiana
A.L. Johnson, Colonel in World War II, cited for bravery
Eugene Hainer, Lincoln, Nebraska, Member of the U.S. House of Representatives, 1893, 1895
K. Keszthelyi, First Lieutenant in World War II, received the Distinguished Service Cross
Frederick Knefler, Brigadier-General in the Civil War

Michael de Kovats, Colonel-Commander of Washington's Cavalry

Géza Mihalótzy, Colonel in the Civil War, organizer of the Lincoln Riflemen in Chicago

László Pásztor, Chairman of the Advisory Board of the Republican Nationalist Committee, 1971

George Pomütz, Colonel in the Civil War, appointed Consul General at St. Petersburg

Nicholas Perczel, Colonel in the Civil War, commanded a brigade, appointed Brigadier-General

Anna M. Rosenberg (Mrs.), Under-Secretary of Defense in the Truman Cabinet; received the Medal of Freedom, 1945, and the Medal of Merit, 1947

Julius Stahel-Számwald, Major General in the Civil War, received the Congressional Medal of Honor

Julius J. Tóth, Captain in World War II, cited for bravery

Charles Zágonyi, Colonel in the Civil War, hero of the famous cavalry charge at Springfield

Music

Dezsö Antalffy-Zsiros, organ virtuoso

Leopold Auer, music educator

Béla Bartók, composer

Sári Biró, pianist

Lajor Bleuer, conductor

George Cziffra, pianist

Julius D'Albert, violinist

Otto Deri, cellist

Ernst V. Dohnányi, composer, conductor, and pianist

Nándor Domokos, conductor

Antal Doráti, conductor and composer

Charles Feleky, conductor (first collector of Hungarian materials in the U.S.A.)

Andor Földes, pianist

Rubin Goldmark, composer

László Halász, conductor

Alexander Harsanyi, violinist, conductor, and professor of music

Otto Herz, pianist

Miklós Ivanich, pianist

Emery Kálmán, composer

Duci Kerékjártó, violinist

Edward Kilényi, pianist

Tibor Kosma, pianist

Gábor Magyar, cellist

Erwin Nyiregyházi, violinist

Carla Ordassy, soprano (Metropolitan Opera)

Eugene Ormándy, conductor

Fritz Reiner, conductor

Gábor Rejtö, cellist

Edward Reményi, violinist

Miklós Rózsa, composer (especially of famous scores for movies

Zoltán Rozsnyai, conductor

György Sandor, pianist

János Schoz, cellist

Miklós Schwalb, pianist

Antal Seidl, conductor

Albert Sirmay, composer

Janos Starker, cellist

Tibor Szasz, pianist

George Szell, conductor

Joseph Szigeti, violinist

Edward Zerdahelyi, pianist

Science

Franz Alexander, authority on the behavioral sciences

Béla Alexay, engineer, twice winner of the Charles A. Coffin Prizes

George V. Békessy, Nobel Prize winner in Medicine and Physiology, 1961

Helen Beretvás, senior researcher of the Standard Oil Research Laboratory

Tibor de Cholnoky, authority on cancer

Ernest Csendes, research chemist

Adolph Eichorn, authority on soils and fertilizers

Jules Freund, received a citation for his work on TB serums

Denis Gábor, Nobel prize winner in physics, 1971

Gabor Galambos, acoustical scientist

Joseph Galambos, designer of the model T. for the Ford Factory

Carl Goldmark, developer of colored television

Max Goldzicher, authority on endocrinology

István Hegedüs, researcher in cardiology, developed the Carotid Compression Test

Theodore von Karman, renowned authority on aerodynamics

Paul Kaufman, citation for immunization against pneumococcus

Gábor Kron, researcher in film synchronization

David E. Lilienthal, Chairman of the U.S. Atomic Energy Commission

John von Neumann, physicist and mathematician, Fermi award winner

Tivadar Puskás, close collaborator of Edison

Erwin Raisz, engineer, authority on mapping

Frederick S. Reiss, authority on leprosy

Béla Schick, introduced the Schick Test measuring immunity from diphtheria

Michel Somogyi, introduced the Somogyi Test to diagnose diabetes

Leo Szilárd, physicist, Atom for Peace Award winner

Albert Szent-Györgyi, Nobel Prize winner in medicine and phisiology, 1937

Géza de Takáts, vascular surgeon

Mária Telkes, authority on solar energy (MIT)

Edward Teller, physicist, Fermi Award winner, 1962

Max Thoerek, authority on surgical technique

Clara Torda, authority on neuromuscular transmission

László Zechmeister, author of textbook on organic chemistry

Eugene Wigner, Nobel Prize winner in Physics, 1963, also a winner of the Atom for Peace Award and the Fermi Award

Sports

Paul Apostol, fencing, U.S. College Champion

Pál Benkö grandmaster of chess and U.S. open champion

Andrea Bodó, gymnast

János Bordy, water polo

Julius Boros, gold, U.S. Open Champion

János Chaplar, distance runner

Béla Csajagh, fencing master

Larry Csonka, football

Joseph Deutsch, water polo

Gyula Dobay, swimmer, Hungarian junior champion

Csaba Elthes, fencing master

Andy Farkas, football

Sandor Ferenczy, women's track coach

Dezső Frigyes, boxing

Andreas Gál, table tennis, U.S. Champion, 1958

Charlie Gogolak, football

Peter Gogolak, football

János Gorkoi, distance runner

Olga Gyarmaty, women's track, world champion

George Halas, owner & trainer (football)

Jenö Hámori, fencing

Istvan Hernec, canoist, Hungarian junior champion

Zoltán Hoszpodár, water polo

Mihály Iglói, men's track coach

György Jekelfalussy-Piller, fencing, world saber champion

Lászlo Jeney, water polo

György Kárpáti, water polo

Attila Keresztes, fencing

Anton Kocsis, boxing

Margit Korondi, gymnast

Thomas Kovács, swimmer, All-American Swimming Team

Tibor Machan, rowing coach

Daniel Magay, fencing

László Magyar, swimmer, world champion, Junior Division

Miklos Martin, water polo

Joe Medwick, baseball

Gábor Nagy, water polo

Martha Nagy, gymnast

Steve Nagy, bowling, U.S. champion, 1959

Joe Namath, football

Tibor Nyilas, fencing, world champion, seven times saber champion of the U.S.A.

Sándor Orbán, high jump

Szusza Ördögh, swimmer, Olympic swimmer, silver medal

Bob Pástor, boxing, U.S. champion, 1939

Károly Pesthy, fencing master

Paul Pesthy, fencing, second place in U.S. college championship

Géza Pókay, fencing master

Béla Rerrick, fencing, Olympic Champsion, silver medal

Csilla Rózsa, tennis

Joseph Sakovich, fencing, Olympic champsion, silver medal

George Santelli, fencing master

Stephen Serényi, Liberty distance runner

Don Shula, football

Ferenc Sipos, marathon, U.S. champion

Sándor Szábo, wrestling

Kató Szöke, swimmer, Olympic champion

Lászlo Tábori, distance runner

Attila Takács, gymnast

Alice F. Tarnay, women's track, Hungarian champion

Louis Thesz, wrestling

Zoltán Török, rowing coach

Mária Tóth, gymnast, first prize in college ground gymnastics

Daniel Végh, table tennis, European champion

Ervin R. Végh, water polo

George Worth, fencing

Ervin Zádor, water polo

Ödön Zombori, wrestling, Olympic champion

Victor Zsufka, pole vaulter

Miscellaneous

Mike Hargitay, Mr. Universe, 1950

Éva Kovách, first alternate of World Queen of Posture and Physical Fitness, Florida, 1966

Judith M. Reményi, Miss U.S.A., 1966

HUNGARIAN AMERICAN PUBLICATIONS

Alkotó Magyar (Creative Hungarian). Irregular. Editor: Geza Korda. Publisher: G.P.O Box 174, New York, N.Y. 10001.

The American Association for the Study of Hungarian History. Newsletter. Irregular. Editor: Thomas Sakmyster, Department of History, University of Cincinnati, Cincinnati, Ohio 45221. Publisher AASHH.

The American Hungarian Review, 1963. Quarterly, cultural: literature, art, science; cir.: 1,000. Publisher and editor: Leslie Könnyü. 5410 Kerth Rd., St. Louis, Missouri 63128.

Amerikai Magyar Élet (American Hungarian Life), 1959. Weekly, Sat., general news; cir.: Publisher and Editor: Lajos Halmagyi Adam. 3636 N. Paris Avenue, Chicago, Ill. 60634.

Amerikai Magyar Népszava (American-Hungarian People's Voice), 1901. Daily except Sun., general news; cir.: 8,548. Editor: Zoltan Gombos. 1736 E. 22nd St., Cleveland 14, Ohio 44114. Managing editor N.Y. Office: Izso Szekely. 305 East 80th Street, New York City, N.Y.

Amerikai Magyar Szó (Hungarian-American Word), 1952. Weekly, general news; cir.: 2,800. Editor: Alex Rosner. 130 East 16th Street, New York, N.Y. 10003.

Amerikai Magyar Világ (American Hungarian World). Weekly, cir.: 7,633. Editor: Zoltan Gombos. Publisher: The Liberty Publishing Co. 1736 East 22nd St., Cleveland, Ohio 44114.

Árpád Akadémiai Értesitö (Bulletin of the Arpad Academy). Irregular. Publisher: Arpad Academy, 1450 Grace Ave., Cleveland, Ohio, OMP 44107.

Baltimore-i Értesitö (Bulletin of the Baltimore Hungarian Society). Monthly. Publisher: Baltimore Hungarian Society, P.O. Box 7416, Baltimore, Md. 21227.

Bethlehemi Hiradó (Bethlehem Hungarian News), 1923. Weekly, general news; cir.: 1,300. Owner and publisher: American Windish and Hungarian Publishing Co. Editor: Stephen Kvochak. 1139 East Third Street, Bethlehem, Pa.

Californiai Magyar Élet (Californian Hungarians' Life), 1957. Bimonthly, literary, illustrated magazine, cir.: 1,500. Publisher and editor:Joseph J. Réthy. 351 W. Broadway, Glendale, California.

California Magyarsag (California Hungarians), 1922. Weekly, cir.: 3,120. Publisher: Zoltán V. Szabados. Editor: Maria Fenyes. 105 S. Western Ave., Los Angeles, California 90004.

Chicagó es Környéke (Chicago and Vicinity), 1906. Weekly, Fri., general news; cir.: 12,210. Publisher and editor: Julius Hovány. 1541 W. Touhy Avenue, Chicago, Illinois 60626.

Detroiti Magyar Ujsag (Detroit Hungarian News). Weekly, cir.: 1,600. Publisher: Karpat Publisher Co. Editor: Zoltán Kótai. P.O. Box 5348, Cleveland, Ohio 44101.

The Eighth Tribe. Twice monthly. Editor: Sándor E. Chomos. Publisher: The Bethlen Press, Imc. P.O. Box 637, Ligonier, Pennsylvania 15658.

Az Ember (The Man), 1927. Weekly, political; cir.: 10,720. Editor: Dr. Zoltán Klár. Publisher: Man Publishing Company, Inc. 100 West 80th Street, New York, N.Y.

Erös Var (Fortress). Publisher: P.O. Box 02148, Cleveland, Ohio 44102.

Értesitö (Bulletin of the Boston Hungarian School and Boy Scout). Irregular. Publisher: Boston Hungarian School, c/o Lajos Koncz, 1463 Beacon St., Brookline, Massachusetts 02146.

Evangeliumi Hirnök (Gospel Messenger), 1909. Monthly, religious. Publisher: Hungarian Baptist Union of America. 748 Fordham Rd., Palm Bay, Florida 32901.

Fáklya (Torch, Hungarian Heritage Society, Newsletter). Irregular. Publisher: Hungarian Heritage Society of Florida. 350 26th Avenue SE, St. Petersburg, Florida.

Fáklyaláng (Torchlight). Political. Editor: Mkhaly Hoka. Publisher: Hungarian October 23rd Movement, Inc. P.O. Box 249 Gracie Station, New York, N.Y. 10028.

Függetlenség (Independence), 1913. Weekly, general news; cir.: 3,600. Publisher and editor: László I. Dienes. 37 Cummings Ave, Trenton, New Jersey.

A Hét (The Week). Weekly, general news. Publisher: 4161 Lorain Ave., Cleveland, Ohio, 44113.

Hiradó (Herald), 1921. Weekly, general news; cir.: 3,950. Publisher and editor: Laszlo I. Dienes. 303 Maple Street, Perth Amboy, New Jersey, 08861.

Hirünk a Világban (Our World News). Editor: István Csicsery-Rónay. Publisher: Occidental Press. P.O. Box 1005, Washington, D.C.

Hungarian Studies Newsletter. Irregular. Editor: Béla C. Máday. Publisher: Hungarian Research Center, American Hungarian Studies Foundation. P.O. Box 1084, New Brunswick, New Jersey 08903

Itt-Ott (Here and There). Monthly. Editor: Lajos Éltető. P.O. Box 112, Ada, Ohio. 45810.

Jersey Hiradó (Jersey Hearld), 1920. Weekly, Thursday, general news; cir.: 1,465. Publisher and editor: Nicholas D. Gerenday. 27 Hancock Avenue, Trenton, New Jersey.

Kárpát (Charpat). Irregular. Cir.: 1,000. Editor: Zoltán Kótai. Publisher: Karpat Publishing Co., Inc. P.O. Box 5348, Cleveland, Ohio 44102.

Katolikus Magyarok Vasárnapja (Catholic Hungarians' Sunday), 1894. Weekly, general news, religious; cir.: 5,000. Editor: Father Gabriel Takacs, OFM. Publisher: Catholic Publishing Company. 517 South Belle Vista Avenue, Youngstown, Ohio 44509.

Képes Magyar Világhiradó (Illustrated Hungarian World Review). Monthly. Editors: Lajos Füry and Judith Petress. 9527 Madison Ave., Cleveland, Ohio 44102.

Kerecsen (Falcon). Newsletter, 1974. Quarterly. Publisher and Editor: Dezsö Gyurky, 3311 Cardinal Ave., Ann Arbor, Michigan 48104.

Központi Értesitö (Central Bulletin). Irregualr. Editor: Gabor Bodnar. Publisher: Hungarian Scout of America, P.O. Box 85, Garfield, N.J. 07026.

Lorain es Vidéke (Lorain and Vicinity), 1914. Weekly, general and social news; cir.: 885. Publisher and editor: Louis P. Bodnar. 1826 East 28th Street, Lorain, Ohio 44055.

Magyar Bányászlap (Hungarian Miners' News). Biweekly; cir.: 1,150. Editor: Andrew Fay Fisher. 7907 West Jefferson Avenue, Detroit, Mich.

Magyar Cserkész (Hungarian Scout Magazine). Monthly. Editor: Gabor Bodnar. Publisher: Hungarian Scout of America, P.O. Box 85, Garfield, New Jersey 07026.

Magyar Egyház (Magyar Church), 1922. Monthly, except June-July and Aug.-Sept., when bimonthly; religious Organ of the Hungarian Reformed Church in America. Publisher: Magyar Egyhaz Publishing Company. Editor-in-chief: Zoltán Béky, Bishop; editor: Dr. Andrew Harsányi, c/o Bethlen Freedom Press, Ligonier, Pennsylvania 15658.

Magyar Hirnök (Magyar Herald), 1910. Weekly, cir.: 4,750. Publisher and editor: László I. Dienes (222 Amboy Ave., Metuchen, N.J.) 216 Somerset Street, P.O. Box 27, New Brunswick, New Jersey 08901.

Magyar Szabadsagharcos (Hungarian Freedom Fighters), 1961. Monthly, political. Pub: Hung. Freedom Fighters Fed. Ed: G. Lovas, P.O. Box 214 Union City, New Jersey.

Magyar Ujság (Hungarian News), 1935. Monthly, general news. Publisher: Pannonia Press, Inc. Editor: György Ratty. 518 Octavia Street (2) San Francisco, California 94102.

Magyarság (Hungarian People), 1925. Weekly, biweekly in July and Aug., general news; cir.: 4,000. Publisher and editor: Eugene Szebedinszky. 200 Johnston Ave., Pittsburgh, Pennsylvania, 15207.

Napnyugat (Western Region). Monthly, cir.: 3,120. Editor: Lorant Zas. Publisher: Maria Fenyes, 105 S. Western Ave., Los Angeles, Calif. 90004.

Nemzeti Figyelö (National Observer). Monthly. Editor and publisher: István Szatmári, P.O. Box "H", Garfield, N.J. 07026.

New Yorki Magyar Élet (New York Hungarian Life). Weekly, cir.: Editor: András László. 6 Alcina Ave., Toronto, Ontario, Canada M6G 2E8.

Ötágú Sip (Ocharine). Monthly. Publisher: 364 Somerset St., New Brunswick, N.J. 08901.

Pátria, The Newspapers of Young Hungarians. Cir.: 5,000. Editor: Lel Somogyi: P. O. Box 2727, Cleveland, Ohio 44111.

Reformatusok Lapja (Calvin Synod Herald). Monthly, religious; cir.: 4,000. Editor: Rev. Francis Vitez. Publisher: Calvin Synod - United Church of Christ, 493 Amboy Ave., Perth Amboy, N.J. 08861.

St. Louis és Vidéke (St. Louis and Vicinity), 1913. Biweekly, general news; cir.: 6,000. Publisher and editor: Louis B. Denes. 1016 Moorlands Dr., St. Louis, Missouri 63117.

The Southwest Journal, 1914. Weekly, Thurs., general news; cir.: 16,134. Publisher and editor: Mrs. Ernest Palos, 8502 West Jefferson Avenue (17), Detroit, Michigan.

Studies for a New Central Europe. Irregular. Publisher: Mid-European Research Institute. P.O. Box 116 F.W. Sta. Mount Vernon, N.Y. 10552.

Sumir Hiradó (Sumerian Messenger). Monthly. Publisher and Editor: György Zászlós-Zsóka, P.O. Box 1486, Cupertino, California 95014.

Szabad Sajtó (Free Press), 1909. Weekly, general news; cir.: 3,600. Publisher and editor: László I. Dienes (215 Third Street, Passaic, New Jersey) 216 Somerset St., P.O. Box 27, New Brunswick, New Jersey 08901.

Szabadság (Liberty), 1891. Daily except Sunday, general news; cir.: 19,893. Editor: Zoltán Gombos. Publisher: The Liberty Publishing Company, 173 East 22nd Street, Cleveland, Ohio 44114.

Szittyakürt (Chythian Horn). Monthly. Publisher: Hungaria Szabadsagharcos Mozgalom, P.O. Box 534, Edgewater Branch, Cleveland, Ohio 44107.

A Sziv (The Heart), 1915. Monthly, religious. Publisher: Hungarian Jesuit Fathers. Editor: Rev. Rochus Radányi. P.O. Box 500, Shrub Oak, New York 10588.

Tájékoztató (Information), 1961. Bimonthly, general news and group interests. Publisher: World Federation of Hungarian Jews, 311 West 23rd Street (Cornish Arms Hotel), New York, New York.

Testvériség (Fraternity), 1923. Monthly, fraternal; cir.: 32,000. Organ of and publisher: The Hungarian Federation of America. Editor: Officers of the Federation, 3216 New Mexico Avenue, Washington, D.C. 20016.

Transsylvania. Monthly, cir.: 500. Editor: Editorial Staff. Publisher: American Transsylvanian Federation, P.O. Box 1671, Grand Central Station, New York, New York 10017.

Tudositó Bulletin (News Bulletin), 1974. Monthly, Publisher: American Hungarian Federation, 3216 New Mexico Ave., Washington, D.C. 20016.

Az Ujság (The News), 1921. Weekly, general news; cir.: 2,800. Publisher and editor: Zoltán Kótai. P.O. Box 5348, Cleveland, Ohio 44101

Új Szárnyak (New Wings). Editor: Frigyes Hefty Jr., 734 Ashland Ave., Santa Monica, California 90405.

Új Vilag (New World). Editor: Ference Orban, 5017 Melrose Ave., Los Angeles, California 90038.

Vezetök Lapja (Leaders' Periodical). Irregular. Editor: Gábor Bognár. Publisher: Hungarian Scout of America, P.O. Box 85, Garfield, New Jersey 07026.

Virrasztó (Vigil-keeper). Quarterly. Editor: István Erdélyi, 45-54 41st Street, Apt. 6E, Long Island City, New York 11104.

William Penn, 1918. Semi-monthly, fraternal, alternate issues in Hungarian and English. Publisher and organ of: William Penn Fraternal Association. Managing editor: Julius Macker, 436-442 Fourth Avenue, Pittsburgh, Pennsylvania.

Wisconsin Magyarság (Wisconsin Hungarians), 1924. Weekly, cir.: 18,700. Publisher and editor: Charles Klein, 609 North Plankinton Ave., Room 508, Milwaukee, Wisconsin 53203.

HUNGARIAN SOCIETIES IN AMERICA

CALIFORNIA

Altadena
Hungarian Engineers Circle.
702 W. Harriet St.

Bloomington
South Californian Hungarian
Club
19006 San Bernardino St.

Gardena
William Penn Association
P.O. Box 2289.

Glendale
Fine Arts Association (Hungarian)
P.O. Box 4051.

Hollywood
American Hungarian Social
Service
19443 Magnolia Blvd.

Hungarian Freedom Fighters'
World Federation in California
P.O. Box 1263.

Magyar Melodiak Radio Club
11621 Keswick St.

Los Angeles
American Hungarian Association
South California Division
P.O. Box 74204.

California Hungarian Freedom
Fighters Association
P.O. Box 34058.

Condor Hungarians Soccer Club
1975 W. Washington Blvd.

Csardas Children's Folk Dance
Group
1975 W. Washington Blvd.

Hungarian Aid Club
1526 Crenshaw Blvd.

Hungarian American Culture
Association
1004 Echo Park Ave.

Hungarian American Ladies
Aid Society
1526 Crenshaw Blvd.

Hungarian Artists' Association
531 So. Fairfax Ave.

Hungarian Catholic Women's
Association
3705 Woodlawn Ave.

International Institute of Los
Angeles (Hungarian Section)
435 So. Boyle Ave.

Karpatok Hungarian Folk Dance
Association
1751 No. Stanley Ave.

Körösi Csoma Association
P.O. Box 45143.

Los Angeles Hungarian House
1975 W. Washington Blvd.

Los Angeles Hungarian Students'
Association
P.O. Box 67642.

M.H.B.K.
P.O. Box 74204.

"Margitsziget" Club
P.O. Box 75749.

Marta Circle
1101 W. Florence Ave.

Melody Radio Club
6654 Hough St.

Napnyugat Author's Circle
105 So. Western Ave.

Old Hungarian American Family
of California
1975 W. Washington Blvd.

St. Stephen Roman & Greek
Catholic Sick Benefit Association
3715 Woodlawn Ave.

Shelters for Israel
735 No. Highland Ave.

Szent Istvan R.K. Women's
Club
3705 Woodlawn Ave.

Monterey
    Monterey American Hungarian
    Club
    P.O. Box 1189.

Pasadena
    Szent Istvan Hungarian R.C.
    Society
    2595 Las Lunas Ave.

San Diego
    San Diego Hungarian House
    3951 Boone St.

San Francisco
    Pannonia Athletic Club
    724 15th Ave.

    San Francisco Hungarian House
    625 Polk St.

Santa Monica
    Grof Zrinyi Miklos Literary
    Circle
    P.O. Box 655.

    M.H.B.K. Division of Santa
    Monica
    P.O. Box 644.

Upland
    Finta Sandor Literary and Art
    Society
    704 Camphor Way.

COLORADO

Denver
    Hungarian Catholic League of
    America (Group of Denver)
    2931 Hudson St.

    Hungarian Soccer Club
    2623 West 27th Ave.

Golden
    American Hungarian Society
    of Colorado
    705 Joyce St.

CONNECTICUT

Bridgeport
    M.H.B.K. (Hungarian Veterans'
    Federation)
    827 North Ave.

    Pannonia American Hungarian
    Club
    78 Grove St.

Hartford
    Hungarian Club
    P.O. Box 184, Station A.

DISTRICT OF COLUMBIA

Washington
    American Hungarian Cultural
    Center
    P.O. Box 3702, Georgetown
    Station.

    American Hungarian Federation
    3216 New Mexico Ave., N.W.

    Hungarian American Cultural
    Club
    206 Dupont Circle Bldg.

    Hungarian Reformed Federation
    of America
    Kossuth House
    3216 New Mexico Ave., N.W.

FLORIDA

Miami
    Hungarian American Cultural
    Clug
    39th St. and 2nd Ave.

    Hungarian American Jewish
    Club
    1702 Alton Rd.,
    Miami Beach

    Hungarian Kossuth Recreation
    Hall
    2230 N.W. 14th St.

St. Petersburg
    Hungarian Heritage Society of
    Florida
    350 26th Avenue SE.

Sarasota
    Petőfi Cultural Association
    2126 Olentary St.

ILLINOIS

Chicago
    Hungarian Cultural Association
    3313 N. Clark.

    First Hungarian Roman & Greek
    Catholic Ladies Sick Benefit of
    Burnside
    9737 Woodlawn

    First Hungarian Social and Sick
    Benefit Association
    2142 N. Clifton Ave.

    Hungarian Club of Chicago
    7732 Saginaw Ave.

    Hungarian Reformed Men's and
    Ladies' Benefit Association
    12300 So. Indiana St.

Granite City
    Hungarian House Committee
    1729 Maple St.

Highland Park
    Hungarian Society
    1630 Ravine Lane.

Park Ridge
    Hungarian Society
    1109 So. Rose St.

INDIANA

Gary
    The Independent Hungarian Po-
    litical Club
    1164 Pierce St.

South Bend
  Hungarian Catholic League of
  America
  829 West Calvert St.

South Bend Democratic Hungarian
Club
820 W. Indiana St.

Whiting
  Hungarian Sick Benefit & Burial
  Society
  1227 Lakeview St.

MARYLAND

Baltimore
  Baltimore Hungarian Society
  P.O. Box 7416.

MASSACHUSETTS

Boston
  Hungarian Society of Boston
  c/o International Institute
  287 Commonwealth Ave.

MICHIGAN

Detroit
  Hungarian Evangelical Lutheran
  Sick Benefit & Burial Society
  7611 Braile St.

Hungarian Social and Athletic
Club
8005 W. Jefferson.

Petöfi Circle
8124 Burdeno St.

MINNESOTA

St. Paul
  Minnesota Hungarians. International Institute of Minnesota
  1694 Como Ave.

MISSOURI

St. Louis
  Cardinal Mindszenty Foundation
  Box 321, Clayton Branch.

MONTANA

Billings
  World Federation of Hungarian
  Engineers and Architects
  c/o Eugene Padanyi-Gulyas
  248 Avenue F.

NEBRASKA

Omaha
  Hungarian Home
  1623 Cuming St.

NEW JERSEY

Bordentown
  American Hungarian Civic Association
  44 Edgewood Rd., West
  Sylvan Glen.

Clark Township
  Rahway American Hungarian
  Citizens
  Old Raritan Rd.

Garfield
  American Hungarian Citizens'
  League
  21 New Schley St.

Hungarian American Democratic
Club
297 Woodbridge Ave.

Hungarian Freedom Federation,
Inc.
49 Prospect St.

Linden
  Hungarian Round Table Chari-
  table Association
  431 Maple Ave.

Milltown
  Our Lady of Hungary Sick &
  Death Benefit Society
  11 Columbia Ave.

New Brunswick
  American Hungarian Democratic
  Club
  190 Albany St.

  American Hungarian Studies
  Foundation
  177 Somerset St.

  Hungarian American Athletic
  Club
  10 Scott St.

  Lorantffy Zsuzsanna Reformed
  Ladies Society
  c/o Bayard St. Presbyterian
  Church
  22 Schuyler St.

  Hungarian Reformed Church
  Sewing Circle
  745 Hamilton St.

  Our Lady of Hungary Sick &
  Death Benefit Society
  49 Duke St.

  St. Emery Ladies Auxiliary
  745 Hamilton St.

  St. Emery Society
  195 Hamilton St.

Perth Amboy
  Louis Fesellyei Ladies Democratic Club
  424 Alpine St.

South River
  Hungarian Women's Democratic
  Club
  127 Prospect St.

Trenton
  American Hungarian Civic As-
  sociation
  P.O. Box 559.

  Council of American-Hungarian
  Churches & Societies
  511 Horne Ave.

  St. Stephen's Catholic Club
  110 Brown St.

NEW YORK

Buffalo
  Hungarian Freedom Flag Com-
  mittee
  P.O. Box 223.

New York
  Alliance of Free Hungarian Law-
  yers of America
  125 East 2nd St.

  American Hungarian Art Association
  53 West 85th St.

  American Hungarian Jewish
  Youth Cultural Group
  242 West 76th St.

  American Hungarian Library
  and Historical Society
  215 East 82nd St.

  American Hungarian Medical
  Society
  936 Fifth Ave.

American Hungarian Society,
Inc.
P.O. Box 62, Gracie Station

American Hungarian Women's
League
8332 Cornish Ave., Elmhurst
Long Island

American Transsylvanian Federation
P.O. Box 1651, Grand Central
Station

Association of Hungarian Jews
of America
2495 Steinway, Astoria, Long
Island

Association of Hungarian Students in North America
211 East 89th St.

Bereg-Munkács Sick and Benevolent Society
Adolphi Hall
74 Fifth Ave.

B'nai Zion, Hungarian Departments
Secretary General: Hermann
Z. Quittman
Organization Secretary: Bernat
Scherf
Chapter No. 23, Debrecen
and Vicinity
Chapter No. 33, Beszterce and
Vicinity
Chapter No. 34, Kisvárda and
Vicinity
Chapter No. 42, Nagyszöllős
and Vicinity
Chapter No. 46, Debrecen and
Vicinity
Chapter No. 54, Deés and Vicinity

Chapter No. 59, Kassa and Vicinity
Chapter No. 71, Viso and Vicinity
Chapter No. 73, Theodore
Hertzl Lodge
Chapter No. 96, Transylvania
50 West 57th St.

Bronx County Hungarian Democratic Club, Inc.
1044 E. Tremont Ave., Bronx
60.

Central Hungarian Sick Benevolent & Literary Society
225 East 83rd St.

Cistercian Alumni Association
P.O. Box 2633, Grand Central
Station.

Collegial Society of Hungarian
Veterans
27 East 95th St.

Committee for the Hungarian
Liberation
500 Smith St., Brooklyn.

Ehler's Free Masonic Lodge
71 West 23rd St.

Federation of Hungarian American Zionists
President: Miksa Lobl
311 West 23rd St.

Federation of Municipal
Employees of Budapest in Exile
670 West End Ave.

First Hungarian Independent
Lodge
101 West 37th St.

First Hungarian Literary Society
323 East 79th St.

Hungarian Brothers and Sisters
Circle
Árpád Hall
323 East 82nd St.

Hungarian Catholic League of
America
30 East 30th St.

Hungarian Committee
125 East 72nd St.

Hungarian Freedom Federation
50 Central Park West.

Hungarian House
2141 Southern Blvd., Bronx

Hungarian Piarist Alumni Association
4 East 89th St.

Hungarian Sport Federation
111 West 57th St.

Hungarian University Association
211 East 37th St.

Jokai Hungarian Lodge
Yorkville Temple
157 East 86th St.

Kossuth Association
Yorkville Temple
157 East 86th St.

Kossuth Free Masonic Lodge
71 West 23rd St.

Kossuth Odd Fellows Lodge
Adolphi Hall
74 Fifth Ave.

Kossuth Odd Fellows Rebekah
Lodge
Adolphi Hall
74 Fifth Ave.

National Hungarian Democratic
Club
Leaders: Dr. Bela Mark, Mrs.
Malvin Green, Dr. John Tere-
besi
323 East 82nd St.

Nippon Magyar Society
President: Dr. Hiroshi Takeda
P.O. Box 3599, Grand Central
Station.

Pannonia Lodge
Yorkville Temple
157 East 86th St.

Pannonia Rebekah Lodge
13925 31st Rd., Flushing·54,
Long Island

Providence Sick & Benevolent
Society (former Young Peton
Society).
President: Michael Braun
33 West 42nd St.

Szatmár and Vicinity Sick &
Benevolent Society
5 East 196th St., Bronx 68.

Szent Imre American Hungarian Youth Association
350 East 23rd St.

The Kossuth Foundation
211 East 37th St.

The Széchenyi István Society,
Inc.
6 East 65th St.

Transylvania Odd Fellows
Lodge
Yorkville Temple
157 East 86th St.

Transylvania Odd Fellows Rebekah Lodge
Yorkville Temple
157 East 86th St.

Ullmann Adolf Society
Adolphi Hall
74 Fifth Ave.

United Hungarian Jews of America
President: Emery J. Worth
Hotel Milburb
242 West 76th St.

Universal Odd Fellows Lodge
Yorkville Temple
157 East 86th St.

Universal Odd Fellows Rebekah
Lodge
Yorkville Temple
157 East 86th St.

World Federation of Hungarian
Jews
Cornish Arms Hotel
311 West 23rd St.

World Federation of Hungarian
Political Prisoners
125 East 72nd St.

Yorkville Hungarian Democratic Club, Inc.
1528 Second Ave.

OHIO

Akron
    Altar Society of the Sacred
    Heart of Jesus
    734 Grant St.

Hungarian Medical Association
of America
289 Sand Run Rd.

Barberton
    Independent Culture Club
    70 Van Buren Ave.

Cleveland
    Árpád Academy
    1450 Grace Ave.

    Committee of Hungarian Liber-
    ation
    2896 Ludlow St.

    Cuyohoga Hungarian Democra-
    tic Club
    3005 East 130th St.

    Hungarian Association
    1450 Grace Ave

    Hungarian Business & Trades-
    men's Club
    11432 Buckeye Rd.

    Hungarian Central Committee
    of Books and Education
    2826 Washington Ave.

    Hungarian Central Students'
    Book Committee
    2826 Washington Ave.

    Hungarian Freedom Fighters'
    Movement
    8909 Detroit Ave.

    Hungarian Military Order Vitez
    P.O. Box 3937, Shaker Square
    Station.

    Hungarian Society for Self Cul-
    ture
    2059 Fulton Rd.

Pro Hungaria
3218 West 162nd St.

Cincinnati
The American Association for
the Study of Hungarian History
Department of History, University of Cincinnati.

Columbus
Hungarian Home
1501 Parsons St.

Lorain
Hungarian Grand Committee
2133 East 31st St.

Hungarian Ladies Aid Society
3036 Glove Ave.

Youngstown
American Hungarian Federation
of Churches & Societies of
Youngstown
48 Chicago Ave.

PENNSYLVANIA

Bethlehem
United Council of the Bethlehem
and Vicinity Hungarian Churches
and Societies
1339 Delaware Ave.

Coraopolis
Coraopolis Hungarian House
708 4th Ave.

Duquesne
First Hungarian Self Culture
Club
33 North Fifth St.

Homestead
First Hungarian Self Culture
Society
501 East 8th Ave.

Homestead Hungarian Cultural
Society
151 East 8th Ave.

United Hungarian Civic Association
P.O. Box 315.

Johnstown
Hungarian American Citizens'
Club
209 Luther Rd.

Szent Imre Youth Society
491 Sheridan St.

McKeesport
Hungarian Social Club
309 Market St.

McKeesport Hungarian Society
3004 Walnut St.

Philadelphia
American Hungarian Federa-
tion
Rittenhouse Savoy, Room 906.

Lorantffy Zsuzsanna Ladies
Aid Society
1233 Franklin St.

Philadelphia & Vicinity Hungarian Sport Club
4516 Ridge Ave.

Pittsburgh
American Hungarian Social Association
120 Flowers Ave.

Central Committee of Hun-
garian Churches and Societies
4753 Monogahela St.

Daughters of American Hungarian Association
120 Flowers Ave.

Hungarian Independent Singing Society
915 Spring Garden Ave.

Hungarian Professional Society
3912 Dowling St.

Sharon
Hungarian Home
395 East Budd St.

Windber
Hungarian Beneficial Hall
122 8th St.

HUNGARIAN CHURCHES IN AMERICA

Source: Tibor Szy, Hungarians in America.
New York: Hungarian University Association,
Inc., 1963.

Roman Catholic Hungarian Churches

Akron 11, Ohio
    Jézus Szent Szive Church
    734 Grant St.

Allentown, Pennsylvania
    Szent István Church
    510 Union St.

Alpha, New Jersey
    Magyarok Nagyasszonya Church
    5th Ave.

Barberton, Ohio
    Szentháromság Church
    368 Wooster Rd., N.

Beaver Falls, Pennsylvania
    Szent László Church
    612 9th St.

Bethlehem, Pennsylvania
    Kapisztrán Szent János Church
    910 East 4th St.

Bridgeport, Connecticut
    Szent István Church
    330 Spruce St.

    Szent Anna Church
    481 Brewster St.

Brownsville, Pennsylvania
    Jézus Szent Szive Church
    213 Sisth Ave.

Buffalo 7, New York
    Szent Erzsebet Church
    986 Grant St.

Carteret, New Jersey
    Szent Erzsebet Church
    119 Washington Ave.

Danbury, Connectiuct
    Szent Imre Church
    104 Main St.

Dayton, Ohio
    Szent Név Church
    408 N. Conover St.

De Pere, Wisconsin
    St. Norbert Abbey

Detroit, 17, Michigan
    Szent Kereszt Church
    8423 South St.

DeWitt, Michigan
    Angyalos Boldogasszony House
    East Main St.

Doylestown, Pennsylvania
    Pauline Fathers, Our Lady of
    Czenstochowa Church
    P.O. Box 151.

East Chicago 2, Indiana
    Szentháromság Church
    4759 McCooke Ave.

Elyria, Ohio
    Jézus Szent Szive Church
    162 Irondale St.

Fairfield, Connecticut
    Szent Imre Church
    838 Kings Highway

Fairport Harbor, Ohio
    Szent Antal Church
    503 Plum St.

Farrell, Pennsylvania
    Szentháromság Church
    1132 Fruit Ave.

Flint 5, Michigan
    Szent József Church
    1321 Hickory St.

Gary, Indiana
    Szent Imre Church
    720 West 15th St.

Irving, Texas
    Cistercian Fathers
    Cistercian Monastery
    Rt. 2, Box 1.

Johnstown, Pennsylvania
    Szent Imre Church
    416 6th Ave.

Joliet, Illinois
    Szent István Church
    456 Youngs Ave.

Lackawanna 18, New York
    Mária Mennybemenetele Church
    80 Steelawanna Ave.

Leechburg, Pennsylvania
    Nagyboldogasszony Church
    222 Third St.

Lorain, Ohio
    Szent László Church
    1412 East 29th St.

Los Angeles 11, California
    Szent Istvan Church
    3705 Woodlawn Ave.

McKeesport, Pennsylvania
    Szent Istvan Church
    2125 Beacon Ave.

Milwaukee, 3, Wisconsin
    Szent Imre Church
    1917 North 17th St.

Munhail 11, Pennsylvania
    Szent Margit Church
    435 10th Ave.

Newark 2, New Jersey
    Nagyboldogasszony Church
    528 High St.

New Brunswick, New Jersey
    Szent László Church
    215 Somerset St.

New York 28, N.Y.
    Szent István Church
    414 East 82nd St.

Northhampton, Pennsylvania
    Magyarok Nagyasszonya Church
    1293 Newport Ave.

Passaic, New Jersey
    Szent István Church
    223 Third St.

Perth Amboy, New Jersey
    Magyarok Nagyasszonya Church
    697 Cortland St.

Philadelphia 22, Pennsylvania
    Jezus Szent Szive Church
    1403 North Masher St.

Pittsburgh 7, Pennsylvania
    Szent Anna Church
    4735 Chatsworth Ave.

Portage, Pennsylvania
    Keresztelö Szent Janos Church
    900 Johnson Ave.

Portola Valley, California
    Benedictine Fathers of Pannon-
    halma Woodside Priory
    302 Portola Rd.

Roebling, New Jersey
    Nagyboldogasszony Church
    Knickerbocker Ave.

Saint Louis 2, Missouri
    Györedelmes Nagyasszonyunk
    Church
    744 South Third St.

San Bernardino, California
    Szent Terez Church
    923 Congress St.

Santa Ana, California
    Norbertine Fathers of Csorna
    1248 West Bishop St.

South Bend, Indiana
    Magyarok Nagyasszonya Church
    829 W. Calvert St.

    Szent István Church
    1022 West Thomas St.

South Norwalk, Connecticut
    Szent László Church
    25 Cliff St.

South River, New Jersey
    Szent István Vertanu Church
    20 William St.

Toledo 5, Ohio
    Szent István Church
    1880 Genesee St.

Trenton, New Jersey
    210 Genesee St.

Windber, Pennsylvania
    Szüz Maria Church
    705 Somerset Ave.

Woodbridge, New Jersey
    Karmelhegyi Boldogasszony
    Church
    267 Smith St.

Yonkers, New York
    Szent Margit Church
    76 Locust Hill Ave.

Youngstown, Ohio
    Szent Istvan Church
    854 Wilson Ave.

    Magyarok Nagyasszonya Church
    545 N. Belle Vista Ave.

    Franciscan Fathers of Tran-
    sylvania
    517 South Belle Vista Ave.

Greek Catholic Hungarian Churches

Bridgeport, Connecticut
    Szentharomsag Church
    558 Bostwick Ave.

Brownsville, Pennsylvania
    Szent Miklos Church
    302 Third Ave.

Carteret, New Jersey
Szent Illés Church
42 Cook Ave.

Chicago, Illinois
Szentháromság Church
639 East 91st Place

Clarksburg, West Virginia
Szent Miklós Church
313 Charleston Ave.

Cleveland, Ohio
Keresztelő Szent János Church
2779 Ambler Ave.

Szent Mihály Church
4605 Bridge Ave.

Detroit, Michigan
Szent János Church
441 South Harbaugh St.

Gary, Indiana
Szent Mihály Church
410 West 13th Ave.

Homestead, Pennsylvania
Szent Illés Church
333 Ninth Ave.

Lorain, Ohio
Szent Mihály Church
2833 Wood Ave.

McKeesport, Pennsylvania
Urunk Szineváltozása Church
121 Sixth Ave.

Minneapolis, Minnesota
Szent János Church
2215 N. E. Third St.

New Brunswick, New Jersey
Szent József Church
30 High St.

New York, New York
Szent Kereszt Church
312 East 82nd St.

Perth Amboy, New Jersey
Szent Mihály Church
40 Hall Ave.

Toledo, Ohio
Szent Mihály Church
2008 Valentine St.

Trenton, New Jersey
Szent Miklós Church
968 S. Broad St.

Youngstown, Ohio
Szent György Church
1726 Canfield Rd.

Magyar Synod

United Church of Christ

Eastern Classis

Bethlehem, Pennsylvania
526 East 4th St.

Bridgeport, Connecticut
963 Laurel Ave.

Fairfield, Connecticut
79 Birchwood Drive

New York, New York
344 East 69th St.

Passaic, New Jersey
    220 4th St.

Perth Amboy, New Jersey; Ross-
    ville, New York
    493 Amboy Ave.

South Norwalk, Connecticut

    21 Lexington Ave.

Wallingford, Connecticut
    107 South Cherry Street

Woodbridge, New Jersey
    94 James St.

Central Classis

Gary, Pocahontas, Logan, Thorpe,
Pennsylvania
Box 74, Anawalt, West Virginia

Homestead, Pennsylvania
416 Tenth Ave., Munhall, Pa.

Johnstown, Pennsylvania
824 Chestnut St.

Leechburg, Pennsylvania
408 Third St.

Pittsburgh, Pennsylvania
221 Johnston Ave.

Rankin, Springdale, Pennsylvania
415 Butler St.

Vintondale, Pennsylvania
Box 141

Morgantown, West Virginia; Union-
town, Pennsylvania
448 Harding Ave., Morgantown,
Pennsylvania

Lakeside Classis

Ashtabula, Conneaut; Erie, Ohio
849 Harbor St.,
Conneaut, Ohio

Cleveland, Ohio
2856 East Blvd.

Cleveland (West Side), Ohio
1946 West 32nd St.

Columbus, Ohio
365 East Woodrow Ave.

Dayton, Ohio
2301 Hoover Ave.

Detroit, Michigan
8016 Vanderbilt Ave.

Fairport Harbor, Ohio
607 Plum St.

Western Classis

Chicago (West Side), Illinois
8260 W. Foster Ter, Norridge

Chicago (South Side), Illinois
652 East 92nd St.

East Chicago, Indiana
4822 Kennedy Ave.

Flint, Michigan
1817 Delaware Ave.

Gary, Indiana
5147 Carolina St.

Greenwood, Indiana
304 Smith Valley Rd.

Hammond, Indiana
603 Indiana St.

Indiana Harbor, Indiana
3602 Ivy St., Indiana Harbor
East Chicago, Indiana

Joliet, Indiana
7316 Baring Parkway
Hammond, Indiana

Kalamazoo, Michigan
803 Miles St.

Whiting, Indiana
1641 Atchison Ave.

Hungarian Reformed Congregations of the American Synods,

United Church of Christ

Akron, Ohio
860 Coburn Ave.

Bridgeport, Connecticut
697 Clinton Ave.

Buffalo, New York
700 Tonawanda St.

Buffalo (East Side), New York
1450 Clinton St.

Los Angeles, California
1138 West 71st St.

Milwaukee, Wisconsin
812 E. Russell Ave.

Phoenixville, Stowe, Pennsylvania
505 Main St.

San Fernando, California
7011 Goodland Ave.
North Hollywood, California

Hungarian Reformed Church in America

Eastern Classis

Bethlehem, Pennsylvania
139 E. North St.

Carteret, New Jersey
175 Pershing Ave.

Linden, New Jersey
50 Washington, Avenue, Colonia

Perth Amboy, New Jersey
331 Kirkland Place

Roebling, New Jersey
134 Norman Avenue

Trenton, New Jersey
180 Home Avenue

New York Classis

Albany-Schenectady, New York
229 East 82nd St.
New York, New York

Cliffside, New Jersey
375 Riverside Drive
New York, New York

Miami, Florida
601 N. E. 55th Terrace

New York, New York
229 East 82nd St.

Rochester, New York
300 Ridge Rd., Lackawanna, N.Y.

Staten Island, New York
25 Winaut Place
Charleston, Staten Island, N.Y.

Syracuse, New York
700 Tonawanda St.
Buffalo, New York

Warrensville, Connecticut
736 East 85th St., New York, N.Y.

Western Classis

Akron, Ohio
174 Western Ave.

Detroit, Michigan
771 Emmons Blvd.
Lincoln Park, Michigan

Donora, Duquesne, Pennsylvania
1411 Kennedy, Ave., Duquesne

Hollywood, California
751 Crenshaw Blvd., Los Angeles

Ontario, California
704 Camphor Way, Upland, Calif.

Ontario, California
1053 E. 6th St.

Reseda, California
18858 Erwin St.

San Bernardino, California
1562 Wall Ave.

San Francisco, California
119 27th St.

Youngstown, Ohio
925 Mahoning Ave.

United Presbyterian Church in the U.S.A.

Alpha, New Jersey
P.O. Box 233

Aurora, Illinois
176 N. Union St.

Beaver Falls, Pennsylvania
1012 Third Ave.

Brownsville, Pennsylvania
307 Spring St.

Canton, Ohio
1658 Superior Ave., N.E.

Cleveland, Ohio
3586 Lattimore Rd.

Coraopolis, Pennsylvania
River Rd., Perry, Ohio

Daisytown, Pennsylvania
P.O. Box 265

Elizabeth, New Jersey
23 Highland Ave.

Franklin, New Jersey
11 Evans St.

Hammond, Louisiana
Rt. 1, Box 169-A

Lakeland, Florida
P.O. Box 15, Eagle Lake, Fla.

Newark, New Jersey
582 South 12th St.

New Brunswick, New Jersey
22-A Joyce Kilmer Ave.

New York, New York
921 Madison Ave.

Philadelphia, Pennsylvania
300 Ridge Rd., Lackawanna, N.Y.

Sharon, Pennsylvania
1009 Clover St.

South Bend, Indiana
1622 Medora St.

Warren, Ohio
322 Austin Ave.

Wharton, New Jersey
408 Third St., Leechburg, Pa.

Youngstown, Ohio
737 Mahoning Ave.

Presbyterian Church in the U.S.

Albany-Árpádhon, Louisiana
Rt. 1, Box 169-A, Hammond, La.

Reformed Church in America

Manville, New Jersey
235 So. 6th Ave.

New Brunswick, New Jersey
179 Somerset St.

South River, New Jersey
42 Thomas St.

Hungarian Lutheran Churches in the U.S.A.

Bethlehem, Pennsylvania
938 East Fourth St.

Buffalo, New York
1035 Grant St.

Chicago, Illinois
1458 W. Belle Plain Ave.

Cleveland (East), Ohio
2836 East Blvd.

Cleveland (West), Ohio
3245 West 98th St.

New York, New York
357 East 72nd St.

Detroit, Michigan
8141 Thaddeus St.

Pittsburgh, Pennsylvania
161 Hazelwood Ave.

American Hungarian Baptist Church

Alhambra, California
2212-16 S. Fremont Ave.

First Hungarian Evangelist and Reformed Church

Los Angeles, California
1101 W. Florence Ave.

Hollywood, California
1711 Van Nesse Ave.

HUNGARIAN IMMIGRANTS IN THE UNITED STATES
1861-1973

Source: U.S. Department of Justice. Report
of Immigration and Naturalization. June 30,
1973.

1861-1870	7,800
1871-1880	72,969
1881-1890	353,719
1891-1900	592,707
1901-1910*	2,145,266
1911-1920	442,693
1921-1930	30,680
1931-1940	7,861
1941-1950	3,469
1951-1960	75,224
1961-1965	2,591
1966	629
1967	582
1968	534
1969	517
1970	548
1971	488
1972	475
1973	1,008

*Austiran and Hungarian statistics in the U.S.A. have been recorded to-
gether up to 1905.

HUNGARIAN AMERICAN POPULATION IN THE UNITED STATES

Source: U.S. Bureau of the Census. 1970
Census of Population.

	Native Population of Foreign or Mixed Parentage	Foreign Born Population
NEW ENGLAND	1970	1970
Maine	198	42
New Hampshire	305	176
Vermont	446	156
Massachusetts	3,710	1,873
Rhode Island	452	137
Connecticut	15,705	5,936
MIDDLE ATLANTIC		
New York	71,968	43,506
New Jersey	50,189	20,235
Pennsylvania	47,851	14,163
EAST NORTH CENTRAL		
Ohio	60,716	22,228
Indiana	10,638	3,470
Illinois	24,353	11,469
Michigan	29,459	9,743
Wisconsin	8,731	3,717
WEST NORTH CENTRAL		
Minnesota	2,950	791
Iowa	818	189
Missouri	4,167	1,694
North Dakota	1,327	263
South Dakota	424	79
Nebraska	813	247
Kansas	706	232
SOUTH ATLANTIC		
Delaware	677	275

	Native Population of Foreign or Mixed Parentage 1970	Foreign Born Population 1970
Maryland	5,831	1,986
District of Columbia	446	401
Virginia	2,842	972
West Virginia	2,193	738
North Carolina	834	356
South Carolina	349	130
Georgia	1,052	234
Florida	14,506	8,548
EAST SOUTH CENTRAL		
Kentucky	815	288
Tennessee	783	212
Alabama	623	196
Mississippi	249	17
WEST SOUTH CENTRAL		
Arkansas	212	98
Louisiana	940	327
Oklahoma	622	171
Texas	3,680	1,172
MOUNTAIN		
Montana	631	197
Idaho	254	103
Wyoming	214	36
Colorado	2,094	941
New Mexico	533	154
Arizona	2,226	918
Utah	275	119
Nevada	576	175
PACIFIC		
Washington	2,917	1,352
Oregon	1,634	664
California	36,103	21,994
Alaska	140	29
Hawaii	255	87
Total	420,432	183,236

HUNGARIAN REFUGEES ADMITTED TO THE UNITED STATES

Source: U.S. Department of Justice. Report
of the Commissioner of Immigration and Naturalization. June 30, 1973.

Number Admitted	67,869
President's Directive of Dec. 22, 1945	885
Displaced Persons Act of 1948	
Displaced Persons Admitted	12,826
Displaced Persons Adjusting under Sec. 4.	297
German Ethnics	3,504
Refugee Relief Act of 1953	9,659
Act of Sept. 11, 1957 (Secs. 4 & 15)	5,172
Act of July 25, 1958 (Hungarian Parolees)	29,905
Act of Sept. 2, 1958 (Azores & Netherlands Refugees)	5
Act of Sept. 22, 1959 (Sec. 6) (Refugee Relatives)	1
Act of Sept. 22, 1959 (Sec. 6) (Refugee-Escapees)	1,603
Act of Oct 3., 1965 (Conditional Entries by Refugees)	4,001
Act of Nov. 2, 1966 (Cuban Refugees)	11

HUNGARIAN SCHOOLS IN THE UNITED STATES

Cities	Supporting Institutes	Number of Students	No. of Classes Elementary	High	Teachers Prof.	Non-Prof.	Hours

DAILY

Cities	Supporting Institutes	Number of Students	Elementary	High	Prof.	Non-Prof.	Hours
New Brunswick, N.J.	Cath.Ch.	143	2	-	2	-	5
Passaic, N.J.	Cath.Ch.	56	4	-	2	2	5

WEEKLY

Cities	Supporting Institutes	Number of Students	Elementary	High	Prof.	Non-Prof.	Hours
Buffalo, N.Y.	Boy Scout	45	3	1	3	3	2
Barberton, Ohio	Cath.Ch.	30	1	-	1	-	1
Boston, Mass.	Hung.Ass.	35	3	-	3	3	1
W.Cleveland, Ohio	Textbook Board	120	8	-	3	13	2
E.Cleveland, Ohio	Parents	58	4	-	2	2	2
Chicago, Ill.	Boy Scout	Presently being organized					
Chicago, Ill.	Cath.Ch.	20					
Los Angeles, Cal.	Cath.Ch.	35	2	-	2	-	3
Hollywood, Cal.	Boy Scout	21	1	-	1	-	1
New Brunswick, N.J.	Boy Scout	72	6	-	5	1	4
New Brunswick, N.J.	Alumni	45	3(English)	-	5	1	4
New York, N.Y.	School Foundation	81	5	1	3	4	3
New York, N.Y.	Boy Scout	12	secondary education				2
Manville, N.J.	Ref. Ch.	12	1	-	1	-	3
Philadelphia, Pa.	Boy Scout	37	4	-	2	2	1
Perth Amboy, N.J.	Ref. Ch.	6	1	-	-	1	1/2
Pittsburgh, Pa.	Boy Scout	40	2	1	2	2	1
San Francisco, Cal.	Boy Scout	30	2	1	2	-	1
S.Norwalk, Conn.	Ref.Ch.	35	5	-	2	3	2
Woodbridge, N.J.	Hung.Club	14	1	-	1	-	2
Washington, D.C.	Freedom-Fighters Assn.	40	2	-	2	-	2
Yonkers, N.Y.	Boy Scout	38	2	-	2	-	2

Cities	Supporting Institutes	Number of Students	No. of Classes Elementary	High	Teachers Prof.	Non-Prof.	Hours
SUMMER							
S. Sik Boy Scout Park, N. Y.	Boy Scout	22(1973)	3 secondary		2	1	36
Fillmore, N. Y.	Boy Scout	48(1973)	3	-	6	-	30
		Elementary education in Hungarian					
Fillmore, N. Y.	Boy Scout	25	2	-	6	-	30
		Hungarian classes in English					
Los Angeles/ Ont., Cal.	Ref. Ch.	40	1	-	3	2	30
Ligonier, Pa.	Ref. Ch.	52(1973)	2	-	-	6	30

HUNGARIAN LANGUAGE COURSES OFFERED IN AMERICAN UNIVERSITIES

Air Force Language Training Program, Indiana.

American University, Washington, D.C.

Cleveland State University, Ohio.

Colgate University, New York.

Columbia University, New York.

Defense Language Institute.

Foreign Service Institute, Washington, D.C.

Indiana University, Indiana.

Portland State University, Oregon.

Purdue University, Indiana.

Rutgers University, New Jersey.

State University of New York, Stonybrook, New York.

University of California, Berkeley, California.

University of California, Los Angeles, California.

University of Pittsburgh, Pennsylvania.

University of Washington, Washington.

AMERICAN UNIVERSITIES OFFERING COURSES ON EASTERN
EUROPEAN HISTORY, POLITICS, MUSIC, CULTURE, Etc.
with References to Hungary

American University, Washington, D.C.
Boston University, Massachusetts
Brooklyn College, New York
Calgary University
City College, New York
Cleveland State University, Ohio
Colgate University, New York
Colorado University, Colorado
Columbia University, New York
Denver University, Colorado
Duke University, North Carolina
Harvard University, Massachusetts
Illinois University, Illinois
Indiana University, Indiana
Indiana University of Pennsylvania, Pennsylvania
John Caroll University, Ohio
Louisiana State University, Louisiana
Massachusetts Institute of Technology, Massachusetts
Massachusetts University, Massachusetts
Michigan State University, Michigan
Nebraska University, Nebraska
New York University, New York
North Carolina University, North Carolina
Notre Dame University
Ohio Northern University, Ohio
Ohio State University, Ohio
Oregon State University, Oregon

Portland State University, Oregon
Princeton University, New Jersey
Purdue University, Indiana
Rice University
Rutgers University, New Jersey
St. John's University
Slippery Rock College
State University of New York, Stony Brook, New York
Stanford University, California
Union C. & U.
University of Arizona, Arizona
University of California, Berkeley, California
University of California, Davis, California
University of California, Los Angeles, California
University of Kansas, Kansas
University of Michigan, Michigan
University of Minnesota, Minnesota
University of Oregon, Oregon
University of Pittsburgh, Pennsylvania
University of Southern California, California
University of Washington, Washington
Wayne State University
Wesleyan University
Western Reserve University, Ohio
Wisconsin University, Wisconsin
Yale University, Connecticut

HUNGARIAN COLLECTIONS IN AMERICAN LIBRARIES

Bartok Archives, New York, New York.
Boston Public Library, Copley Square, Boston, Massachusetts.
Bridgeport Public Library, 925 Broad St., Bridgeport, Connecticut
Brooklyn Public Library, Grand Army Plaza, Brooklyn, New York
Brown University, Pro vidence, Rhode Island
Buffalo & Erie County Public Library, 25 Nottingham Court, Buffalo, New York
California State Library, Library & Courts Building, Sacramento, California
University of California, Berkeley, California
Carnegie Library, 4400 Forbes St., Pittsburgh, Pennsylvania
Chicago Public Library, 78 East Washington St., Chicago, Illinois
The University of Chicago, Chicago, Illinois
Cincinnati University, Cincinnati, Ohio
Cleveland Museum of Art, 11150 East Boulevard, Cleveland, Ohio
Cleveland Public Library, 325 Superior Ave., Cleveland, Ohio
Columbia University, Morningside Heights, New York, New York
Cornell University, Ithaca, New York
Cayton & Montgomery County Public Library, 215 E. Third St., Dayton, Ohio
Detroit Public Library, 5201 Woodward Ave., Detroit, Michigan
Duke University, Durham, North Carolina
Enoch Pratt Free Library, 400 Cathedral St., Baltimore, Maryland
Georgetown University, 37th and O Street, N.W., Washington, D.C.
Harvard University, Cambridge, Massachusetts
Hoover Institute, Stanford University, Stanford, California
University of Illinois, Urbana, Illinois
Immigration History Research Center, University of Minnesota, 826 Berry Street, St. Paul, Minnesota
Indiana University, 518 N. Delaware St., Indianapolis, Indiana
Indianapolis Public Library, 40 E. St. Clair St., Indianapolis, Indiana
The University of Iowa, Iowa City, Iowa
Johns Hopkins University, Baltimore, Maryland
Kodaly Musical Training Institute, Inc., 525 Worcester St., Wellesley, Massachusetts
Los Angeles County Law Library, 301 W. First St., Los Angeles, California
Louisiana State University, Baton Rouge, Louisiana
University of Michigan, Ann Arbor, Michigan
Milwaukee Public Library, 814 W. Wisconsin Ave., Milwaukee, Wisconsin
Minneapolis Public Library, 300 Nicollet Ave., Minneapolis, Minnesota
Missouri Botanical Garden Library, 2315 Tower Grove Ave., St. Louis, Missouri

National Library of Medicine, Beltsville, Maryland
New York Public Library, Fifth Ave. & 42nd Street, New York City
Newark Public Library, 5 Washington St., Newark, New Jersey
Northwestern University, Evanston, Illinois
University of Notre Dame, Notre Dame, Indiana
Ohio State University, Columbus, Ohio
Princeton University, Princeton, New Jersey
Queensborough Public Library, Springfield Blvd. & L.I. Expressway,
    New York, New York
South Bend Public Library, 122 W. Wayne St., South Bend, Indiana
U.S. Department of Agriculture, Washington, D.C.
U.S. Department of State, Washington, D.C.
U.S. Library of Congress, Washington, D.C.
University of Wisconsin, Madison, Wisconsin
Yale University, New Haven, Connecticut
Yivo Institute for Jewish Research, 1048 Fifth Ave., New York, New York

Notable Private Collections

Louis Szathmary's Archivum. Approximately 20,000 volumes pertaining to
    Hungary. Chicago.
Steven Bela Vardy's collection on Hungarian history. Approximately 6,000
    volumes. Pittsburgh.
Edmund Vasvary's collection. Approximately 375 volumes of manuscripts,
    documents, pamphlets, also a card catalog of 12,000 entries related to
    Hungarians in America. Washington, D.C.

HUNGARIAN NAMED GEOGRAPHIC LOCATIONS IN THE UNITED STATES

Agar, South Dakota
Arpadhon, Louisiana
Balaton, Minnesota
Beky Drive, Trenton, New Jersey
Buda, Illinois
Buda, Texas
New Buda, Iowa (not in use)
Budapest, Georgia (not in use)
Fejervari Park, Davenport, Iowa
Haraszthyville, Wisconsin (not in use)
Imlay, Nevada
Kossuth, Indiana
Kossuth, New York
Kossuth, Mississippi
Kossuth, Pennsylvania
Kossuth Ave., St. Louis, Missouri
Kossuth County, Iowa
Kossuth St., Baltimore Maryland
Kossuth St., Bridgeport, Connecticut
Kossuth St., Bronx, New York
Kossuth St., Cleveland, Ohio
Kossuth St., Columbus, Ohio
Kossuthville, Florida (not in use)
Koszta, Iowa
Rombauer, Missouri
Szantoville, Virginia
Tolna, North Dakota
Vidor, Texas
Zagonyi Park, Springfield, Missouri

Camps named after Hungarian officials in the Civil War: Camp Asboth;
Camp Rombauer, Camp Utassy; Camp Zagonyi and Forth Mihalotzy.

BIBLIOGRAPHY

Books

The American Magyar Review; Magyar Day Issue. August 19, 1937. Pittsburgh: United Magyar Civic Association of Pennsylvania, n.d.

Annals of Cleveland, a Digest and Index of the Newspaper of Events and
Opinions. Vol. 35, Pt. 1, 1852. Cleveland: Work Projects Administration, 1937.

Annals of Cleveland Newspaper Series, Cleveland Foreign Language Newspaper Digest, Hungarian, 1891-1892. Cleveland: Work Projects Administration, 1942.

Annals of Cleveland Newspaper Series, Cleveland Foreign Language Newspaper Digest, Vol. 4, 1938. Cleveland: Work Projects Administration,
1940. Hungarian section: pp. 1-314.

Arnold, G.P. New Buda and the Hungarians. Leon: n.p., 1912.

Bakó, Elemér. Guide to Hungarian Studies. (A Bibliography). Stanford:
Hoover Institute Press, 1973. 2 Vols.

_____. On the Linguistical Characteristics of the American Hungarian.
International Congress of Phonetical Sciences. Fifth Proceeding.
Basel: S. Karger, 1964.

_____. Selective List of Uncatalogued Library of Congress Holdings
Related to Louis Kossuth. Washington, D.C.: Library of Congress,
Slavic and Central European Division, 1969.

Bakó, Elemér and Horváth. J. Michael. Six Hundred Years of Hungarian
University Education. Catalog of the Memorial Exhibit Presented by
the Washington Chapter of the American Hungarian Federation November 4-24, 1967 McKeldin Library Building, University of Maryland Library. College Park: University of Maryland, 1967.

Balogh, J.K. An Analysis of Cultural Organizations of Hungarian-Americans in Pittsburgh and Allegheney County. Ph.D. Dissertation. University of Pittsburgh, 1945.

Bardin, H. The Hungarian in Bridgeport. Bridgeport: University of Bridgeport, 1959.

Bardy de Kovatsi, Rudolph. Adventures of Rudolph Bardy de Kovatsi. Rochester, N.Y.: Press of Lee, Mann & Co., 1855.

Baretski, Charles Allan. American Foreign Relations with East Central Europe, 1823-1867: Hungary and Poland. Ph.D. Dissertation. University of Notre Dame, 1959.

Beynan, Erdman D. Occupational Adjustment of Hungarian Immigrants in an American Urban Community. Ph.D. Dissertation. University of Michigan, 1933.

Birinyi, Louis K. International Justice; Memorandum Submitted by American Citizens of Hungarian Descent . . . to the World Conference of International Justice. Cleveland: n.p., 1928.

Bobula, Ida Miriam. The Hungarian Material in the Library of Congress. Washington, D.C.: Photoduplication Service, Library of Congress, 1953. (Microfilm)

Bognar, Desi K., ed., and Szentpaly, Katalin. Hungarians in America, A Biographical Directory of Professionals of Hungarian Origin in the Americas. 3d ed. Mount Vernon: The AFI Publication, 1973.

Boros, Alexander. "Their New World." A Comparative Study of the Assimilation Patterns of Four Waves of Hungarian Immigration. Honors Dissertation, Kent State University, 1959.

Brace, Emma (Mrs.) Donaldson. The Life of Charles Loring Brace. (Hungarian Reference Library Publication Series, No. 1) New York: Hungarian Reference Library of America, 1941.

Braun, Marcus. Immigration Abuses: Glimpses of Hungary and Hungarians. New York: Pearson, 1906. (Reprinted: San Francisco, R. and E. Research Associates, 1972)

Butosi, John. Church Membership Performance of Three Generations in Hungarian Reformed Churches of Allegheny County, Pennsylvania. Ph.D. Dissertation. University of Pittsburgh, 1961.

California Hungarian Directory, 1973-1974. Los Angeles, California: Californiai Magyarsag, 1973.

Clark, Francis Edwards. Old Homes of New Americans; The Country and the People of the Austro-Hungarian Monarchy and Their Contribution to the New World. Boston and New York: Houghton Mifflin Co., 1913.

Cook, Huldah Florence. The Magyars of Cleveland. Cleveland: Cleveland Americanization Committee, 1919.

Czigány, Magda. Hungarian Literature in English Translation. London: Szepesi-Csombor Circle, 1969.

DiKovics, J. Our Magyar Presbyterians. New York: Board of National Missions of the Presbyterian Church in the United States, 1945.

————. Twenty-five Years of Presbyterian Work among Hungarians in the United States, 1902-1927. New York: Board of National Missions of the Presbyterian Church in the United States, 1927.

Dodds, John W. The Several Lives of Paul Fejös. A Hungarian-American Odyssey. New York: Wenner-Gren Foundation for Anthropological Research, 1973.

Endrey, Eugene. Beg, Borrow and Squeal. New York: Pageant Press, 1963.

Feleky, Antoinette. Charles Feleky and His Unpublished Manuscript. New York: Representative Press, 1938.

Fermi, Laura. Illustrious Immigrants, the Intellectual Migration from Europe, 1930-1941. Chicago: The University of Chicago Press, 1968.

Fishman, Joshua A. Hungarian Language Maintenance in the United States. Bloomington: Indiana University, 1966.

Gáspár, Steven. Four Nineteenth-Century Hungarian Travelers in America. Ph.D. Dissertation University of Southern California, 1967.

Gergely, Emro Joseph. Hungarian Drama in New York; American Adaptations 1908-1940. Philadelphia: University of Pennsylvania, 1947.

Gerster, Árpád. Recollections of a New York Surgeon. New York: P.B. Hoober, 1917.

Gracza, Rezső and Gracza, Margaret. The Hungarians in America. (The in America Series) Minneapolis: Lerner Publications Co., 1969.

Halász de Béky, Iván. A Bibliography of the Hungarian Revolution, 1956. Toronto: University of Toronto, 1963.

Hanzell, Victor E. The Hungarians. New Haven: Human Relations Area Files, Yale University, 1955.

Head, Violet. The 1956 Hungarians; Their Integration into an Urban Community. Ph.D. Dissertation. University of Chicago, 1963.

Héya-Kiss, Mária. Hungarian Classical Literature in the National Union Catalog; a Bibliographical Survey. Thesis. Washington, D.C.: Catholic University of America, Dept. of Library Science, 1953.

Hohenberg, John, ed. The Pulitzer Prize Story. News Stories, Editorials, Cartoons, and Pictures from the Pulitzer Prize Collection at Columbia University. New York: Columbia University Press, 1959.

Hungarian American Foundation; An Association of Americans of Hungarian Ancestry. Detroit: n.p., 1938.

Hungarian Books. (Magyar Könyvek.) A Catalogue of Holdings of the Languages Centre, Metropolitan Toronto Central Library. Toronto: Metropolitan Toronto Library Board, 1971.

Hungarian History and Literature; Classification Schedule, Author and Title Listing, Chronological Listing. Harvard University Library. (Widener Library Shelflist, No. 44) Cambridge: Harvard University Library, 1973.

Hungarian Reference Library, Cards Representing the Holdings in the Hungarian Reference Library. Collection originally owned by Charles Feleky. Washington, D.C.: Library of Congress, Photoduplication Service. (Microfilm)

Hungarian Refugee Students and United States Colleges and Universities. Committee on Educational Interchange Policy. New York: 1957-1958. 2 vols.

Hungarian Republican Club of the City of New York. Proceedings of the Banquet Tendered His Excellency Theodore Roosevelt . . . February 14, 1905. New York: n.p., 1905.

Hungarian Service Book. American Episcopal Church. Diocese of Michigan. Cleveland: Magyar Hirlap, 1915.

Hungarians in America's Making 1850-1921. New York: Frank Bokor, Printer, n.d.

Kalassay, Louis A. The Educational and Religious History of the Hungarian Reformed Church in the United States. Ph.D. Dissertation. University of Pittsburgh, 1939.

Kálnay, Francis. The New American: A Handbook for Necessary Information for Aliens, Refugees and New Citizens. New York: Greenberg Publisher, 1941.

Kautz, Edvin L. The Hungarian Baptist Movement in the United States. Master's Thesis. University of Pittsburgh, 1946.

Kerényi, Caterina Eösze. Poets in Exile: A Comparative Study in Latin and Hungarian Literature. Ph.D. Dissertation. The University of Texas at Austin, 1969.

Klay, Andor. Daring Diplomacy. The Case of the First American Ultimatum. Minneapolis: The University of Minnesota Press, 1957.

Komjáthy, Aladár. The Hungarian Church in America: An Effort to Preserve a Denominational Heritage. Ph.D. Dissertation. Princeton Theological Seminary, 1962.

Konta, Alexander. Naturalized Hungarians, Their Rights and Duties. Delivered under the Auspices of the Hungarian Relief Society at the Public Library, Yorkville Branch, December 7, 1915. New York: Nepszava Printer, 1915.

Könnyü, Leslie. Eagles of Two Continents. St. Louis: The American Hungarian Review, 1963.

_____. A History of American Hungarian Literature. St. Louis: Cooperative of American Writers, 1962.

_____. Hungarians in the U.S.A., An Immigration Study. St. Louis: The American Hungarian Review, 1967.

_____. John Xantus, Hungarian Geographer in America. Köln: American Hungarian Publisher, 1965.

_____. Revisiting St. Louis Catalogue and Biographies of the Hungarian Artists Who Participated in the Art Exhibition of the 1904 St. Louis World Fair. St. Louis: The American Hungarian Review, 1973.

Körösföy, John. Hungarians in America. Cleveland: Szabadság, 1941.

Kósa, John. Land of Choice, the Hungarian in Canada. Toronto: University of Toronto Press, 1957.

Kossuth in New England; A Full Account of the Hungarian Governor's Visit to Massachusetts: With His Speeches and Addresses That Were Made to Him, Carefully Revised and Corrected. Boston: J.P. Jewett & Co., 1852.

Leffler, Andor. Kossuth Episode in America. Ph.D. Dissertation. Western Reserve University, 1949.

Lengyel, Emil. Americans from Hungary. Philadelphia and New York: J.B. Lippincott Co., 1948.

Lotz, John, ed. Hungarian Reader: Folklore and Literature, with Notes. Bloomington: Indiana University, 1962.

Madden, Henry M. Xantus, Hungarian Naturalist in the Pioneer West. Ph.D. Dissertation. Columbia University, 1950.

Major, Mark Imre. American, Hungarian Relations: 1918-1944. Ph.D. Dissertation. Texas Christian University, 1972.

Makár, János. The Story of an Immigrant Group in Franklin, New Jersey, Including a Collection of Hungarian Folk Songs Sung in America. Franklin, New Jersey: Standard Press, 1969.

May, Arthur J. Contemporary American Opinion of the Mid-Century Revolutions in Central Europe. Ph.D. Dissertation. University of Pennsylvania, 1927.

Nadányi, Paul. The "Free Hungary" Movement. New York: The Amerikai Magyar Népszava, Inc., 1942.

Nelson, Ágnes Denman. A Study of English Speech of the Hungarians of Albany, Livingston Parish, Louisiana. Ph.D. Dissertation. Louisiana State University, 1956.

Nemser, William Joseph. An Experimental Study of Phonological Interference in the English of Hungarians. Bloomington: Indiana University, 1971.

_____. The Interpretation of English Stops and Interdental Fricatives by Native Speakers of Hungarian. Ph.D. Dissertation. Columbia University, 1961.

New York (City) Common Council. Report of the Special Committee Appointed to Make Arrangements for the Reception of Gov. Louis Kossuth, the Distinguished Hungarian Patriot. New York: Published by order of the Common Council, 1852.

Piványi, Eugene. Hungarian-American Historical Connections from Pre-
     Columbian Times to the End of the American Civil War. Budapest:
     Royal Hungarian University Press, 1927.

————. Hungarians in American Civil War. Cleveland: Dongo, 1913.

————. Sixty Years Ago. First Hungarian Association for Self-Cul-
     ture of Philadelphia, 1911-15. (English and Hungarian)

————. Webster and Kossuth. Philadelphia: n.p., 1909.

Primes, Agnes. Hungarians in New York. M.A. Thesis. New York: Colum-
     bia University, Faculty of Political Science, 1940.

Quinn, B. David and Cheshire, M. Neil. The New Found Land of Stephen
     Parmeneus, The Life and Writings of a Hungarian Poet, Drowned on
     a Voyage from New Found Land, 1583. Toronto: University of To-
     ronto Press, 1972.

Reisch, Alfred A. The Contribution of Sándor Bölöni Farkas' Study of
     American Democracy and Institutions to Political Perspective of the
     Nineteenth Century Hungarian Age of Reform, 1830-1848. Ph.D.
     Dissertation. Columbia University, 1970.

Revesz, Coloman. Colonel-Commandant Michael de Kovats, Drillmaster
     of Washington Cavalry. Pittsburgh: Verhovay-Fraternal Insurance
     Associations, 1954.

Schuchat, Molly Geiger. Hungarian Refugees in America and Their Coun-
     terparts in Hungary, the Interrelations between Cosmopolitanism
     and Ethnicity. Ph.D. Dissertation. The Catholic University of
     America, 1970.

Select List of References on Louis Kossuth. Washington, D.C.: Library
     of Congress, Division of Bibliography, 1910.

Skinner, P.H. The Welcome of Louis Kossuth Governor of Hungary, to
     Philadelphia, by the Youth, December 26, 1851. Philadelphia: P.H.
     Skinner, 1852.

Souders, David Aaron. The Magyars in America. New York: George H.
     Doran Co., 1922. 119 p. illus. (Reprinted: San Francisco, R. and
     E. Research Associates, 1969).

Stibrán, Teréz D. The Streets Are Not Paved with Gold. Cleveland: Print-
     ing Co., 1961.

Stone, Margaret Lewis. Historical Development and the Use of the Kodaly Music Method and the Orff-Schulwerk Techniques Including Their Present Practice in the U.S.A. Ph.D. Dissertation. Kent State University, 1971.

Szabó, George. Corvinus Manuscripts in the United States, A Bibliography. New York: The Kossuth Foundation Inc., 1960.

Szamek, Pierre Ervin. The Eastern American Dialect of Hungarian: An Analytical Study. Ph.D. Dissertation. Princeton University, 1955.

Szentmiklósy Éles, Géza. Hungarians in Cleveland. M.A. Thesis, John Caroll University, 1972.

Széplaki, Joseph. Bibliography of Louis Kossuth, Governor of Hungary; With Special Reference to His Trip in the United States, Dec. 4, 1851-July 14, 1852; Available in the Ohio University Library. Athens, Ohio: Ohio University Library, 1972.

_____. Doctoral Dissertations Related to Hungary Accepted in the United States and Canada and Bibliographies on Hungary. Athens, Ohio: Ohio University Library, 1974.

Sziklay, Andor. Szabadság; Second Generation Almanac for the American Youth of Hungarian Origin. Cleveland: Szabadsag, 1937, 1938.

Szy, Tibor. Hungarians in America; A Biographical Directory of Professionals of Hungarian Origin in the Americas. New York: Hungarian University Association, 1963.

_____. Hungarians in America; A Biographical Directory of Professionals of Hungarian Origin in the Americas. 2d ed. New York: The Kossuth Foundation, Inc., 1966.

Táborszky, Ottó. The Hungarian Press in America. Master's Thesis. Catholic University of America, 1955.

Tezla, Albert. Hungarian Authors, A Bibliographical Handbook. Cambridge, Mass.: Harvard University Press, 1970.

Trautmann, Fredrick William Edward. Louis Kossuth's Audience Adapta-

tation in His American Speaking Tour, 1851-1852. Ph.D. Dissertation. Purdue University, 1966.

United Nations. Report of the Special Committee on the Problems of Hungary. New York: United Nations, 1957.

United Nations. General Assembly. Further Report on the Problem of
Hungarian Refugees. Submitted by the High Commissioner, 1958.

United States. Congress. House. Recording Admission of Certain Hungarian Refugees. Report from Committee on Judiciary to accompany
H.R. 11033, July 10, 1958. Washington: U.S. Government Printing
Office, 1958. (Senate reports on public bills, 85th Congress, no.
1817)

United States. Congress. Senate. Affairs of Hungary, 1849-1850. Message from the President of the United States, Transmitting Correspondence with A. Dudley Mann (1849-1850) in Response to Senate
Resolution No. 85, of December 7, 1909, Relating to Affairs of Hungary. Washington: U.S. Government Printing Office, 1910. (61st
Congress,. 2nd session, Senate)

United States. Congress. Senate. Committee on the Judiciary. Emigration of Refugees and Escapees. Report of the Committee on the Judiciary, made by its Sub-Committee to Investigate Problems Connec-
ted with the Emigration of Refugees and Escapees, pursuant to S.
Res. 168, 84th Congress, 2d Session, as extended by S. Res. 84,
85th Congress. Washington: U.S. Government Printing Office, 1957.
(85th Congress, 1st session. Senate. Report, 129)

United States. Laws, statutes, etc. H.R. 11033 Act to Authorize Creation of Record of Admission for Permanent Residence in Case of Certain Hungarian Refugees. Approved July 25, 1958. Washington: U.S.
Government Printing Office, 1958. (Public laws, 85th Congress, no.
559).

United States. President's Committee for Hungarian Refugee Relief. Report
to the President. Washington: U.S. Government Printing Office, 1957.

United States. President's Committee for Hungarian Refugees Relief. Out-
line of Organization and Work of President's Committee for Hungarian
Refugee Relief in Assisting in Resettlement of Hungarian Refugees.
Washington: U.S. Government Printing Office, 1957.

Vasady-Nagy, Andor, ed. Cleveland Hungarian Business Directory. (Cleveland és Környéke Magyar Vonatkozású Vállalkozásainak Cimtára és
Kézi Telefonkönyve). Cleveland: Rajkai László, 1967.

Vasváry, Edmund. Linconln's Hungarian Heroes. Washington, D.C.: The Hungarian Reformed Federation of America, 1939.

Walsh, Connie and Széplaki, Joseph. Bibliography on Béla Bartók. Available in the Ohio University Main and Music Library. Athens, Ohio: Ohio University Library, 1972.

Weinstock, S. Alexander. The Acculturation of Hungarian Immigrants: A Social-Psychological Analysis. Ph.D. Dissertation. Columbia University, 1962.

Zeisler, Alexander. Conversational Hungarian. New York: Emil Nyitray, 1907.

Articles

Agárdi, Ferenc. "A Hungarian General in Lincoln's Service." The New Hungarian Quarterly, Vol. 4, No. 10 (April-June, 1963), pp. 155-157.

Bakó, Elemér. "Louis C. Sólyom; Collector of Languages." The Quarterly Journal of the Library of Congress, Vol. 22, No. 2 (April, 1965), pp. 105-118.

Bessey, E.A. "American-Hungarian Foundation Library." Science, Vol. 62 (December 11, 1925), pp. 536-537.

Beyon, Erdmann D. "The Hungarians of Michigan." Michigan Historical Magazine, Vol. 21 (January, 1937), pp. 89-102.

————. "Occupational Succession of Hungarians in Detroit." American Journal of Sociology, Vol. 39 (March, 1934), pp. 600-610

————. "Social Mobility and Social Distance Among Hungarian Immigrants in Detroit." American Journal of Sociology, Vol. 41 (January, 1936), pp. 424-434.

"Bibliography of L. Könnyű's Publications in English, French, German, Spanish and Hungarian." The American Hungarian Review, Vol. 11, Nos. 3-4 (1973), pp. 3-33.

Brown, Vonnie R. "Louisiana Magyar" Viltis, Vol. 32, No. 4 (December, 1973), pp. 5-10.

Claghorn, Katherine H. "Slavs, Magyars and Others in the New Immigration." Charities and Commons, Vol. 13 (December 3, 1904), pp. 199-205.

Duggan, Stephen. "The Hungarian Reference Library of New York." Hungarian Quarterly, Vol. 15, No. 2 (Summer, 1939), pp. 364-367.

"Editors in Exile: Amerikai Magyar Népszava, a Hungarian Daily." Time, Vol. 51, (January 21, 1948), p. 71.

Farkas, Zoltán J. "The Challenge of the Name America." Names, Vol. 13, No. 1 (March, 1965), pp. 11-18.

_____. "Hungarian City and County Names in the United States." Names, Vol. 19, No. 2 (June, 1971), pp. 141-143.

Foltinyi, Stephen. "What Did Pal Fejös Give to the Anthropologists of the World?" The Hungarian Quarterly, Vol. 5, No. 1-2 (April-June, 1965), pp. 172-176.

Gleitman, Henry and Greenbaum, Jos J. "Attitudes and Personality Patterns of Hungarian Refugees." Public Opinion Quarterly, Vol. 25, No. 3 (Fall 1961), pp. 351-365.

"Hungarian Invasion." Saturday Review of Literature, Vol. 142 (October 16, 1926), pp. 434-435.

"Italian, Slavic, and Hungarian Unskilled Immigrant Laborers in the United States." United States Labor Bureau Bulletin, Vol. 15 (September, 1907), pp. 403-486.

Kósa, John. "A Century of Hungarian Emigration, 1850-1950." American Slavic and East European Studies, Vol. 16 (December, 1957), pp. 501-14.

_____. "The Early Immigrants: Hungarians in the U.S.A. in the Nineteenth Century." Hungarian Quarterly, Vol. 7 (1941), pp. 247-253.

_____. "Hungarian Immigrants in North America: Their Ecology and Residential Mobility." Canadian Journal of Economics and Political Science, Vol. 22 (1956), pp. 358-370.

McLaughlein, Allen. "Hebrew, Magyar and Levantine Immigration." Popular Science, Vol. 65 (September, 1904), pp. 438-440.

Magyar, Gustav, pseud. "The Hungarian-American Society, 1945-1949." The Hungarian Quarterly, Vol. 4, No. 1-2 (January-April, 1963), pp. 115-119.

Marchbin, Andrew A. "Early Emigration from Hungary to Canada." Slavonic and East European Review, Vol. 13 (July, 1934), pp. 127-137.

_____. "Hungarian Activities in Western Pennsylvania." Western Pennsylvania Historical Magazine, Vol. 23 (1940), pp. 163-174.

Paikert, Géza. "Hungarian Reference Library in America." Hungarian Quarterly, Spring 1941, pp. 174-177.

Pink, Louis. "The Magyars in New York." Charities and Commons, Vol. 13 (December 3, 1904), pp. 262-263.

Reményi, József. "Hungarians in the United States." Journal of English and German Philology, Vol. 36 (October, 1937), pp. 551-552.

Roucek, J.S. "Hungarians in America." Hungarian Quarterly, Vol. 3 (1937), pp. 358-366. Also published in Brown, F.J. and Roucek, J.S. One America. New York: Prentice Hall, 1945.

Rown, Edmund C. "The Academy's Program for Placement of Hungarian Scientists." New Report, January-February, 1958, p. 5.

Schaeffer, C.E. "Magyars in Hungary and America." Missionary Review of the World, Vol. 38 (May 1915), pp. 367-368.

Sebestyén, Endre. "The Magyars in America." Hungarian Quarterly, Vol. 7 (1941), pp. 228-246.

Shipman, Andrev J. "Hungarian Catholics in America." Catholic Encyclopedia, Vol. 7 (1913), pp. 545-547.

Soskis, Philip. "The Adjustment of Hungarian Refugees in New York." International Migration Review, Vol. 2 (Fall 1957), pp. 40-46.

Steiner, A. "Hungarian Immigrant." Outlook, Vol. 74 (August 29, 1903), pp. 1040-1044.

Vasváry, Edmund. "Lincoln and the Hungarians." William Penn Association Monthly. 12 articles, November, 1961-July 1964.

Wagner, Francis, "The Start of Cultural Exchanges between the Hungarian Academy and the American Philosophical Society, 1834-1857." Hungarian Quarterly, Vol. 5, Nos. 1-2 (1965), pp. 90-97.

Wilson, Lillian Mary. "Some Hungarian Patriots in Iowa." The Iowa Journal of History and Politics, October, 1913, pp. 479-516.